INSPIRED TO
STITCH

THE CREATIVE EMBROIDERY COURSE

Dancers with Shadows

Lilies, a panel
hanging by the author
44 x 58in (1.12 x 1.47m)

INSPIRED TO STITCH

THE CREATIVE EMBROIDERY COURSE

WENDY LEES

A David & Charles Craft Book

Illustrations are by the author
unless otherwise credited

Vienna

British Library Cataloguing in Publication Data
Lees, Wendy
    Inspired to stitch: the creative embroidery course. – (A
David & Charles craft book).
    1. Embroidery
    I. Title
    746.44

    ISBN 0-7153-9499-1

Typeset by ABM Typographics Hull
and printed in Italy
by OFSA SpA
for David & Charles plc
Brunel House   Newton Abbot   Devon

CONTENTS

Squares and Stripes
by Constance Howard.
An exploration of colour
using card strips wrapped
with perlé threads
16¹/₂in (42cm) square

INTRODUCTION

Inspired to Stitch is designed to help and encourage the use of your own ideas and feelings as a starting-point in designing embroidery. We are all individuals, we lead our own lives, and we each have our particular interests and enthusiasms. If these are at the heart of the work we produce, it will then be truly creative and have a personal value. Explaining how to set about such an approach is the main purpose of the book.

We begin by tackling a series of exercises in the use of simple and well-known stitches and a variety of threads and fabrics. These produce very different and lively results as you can see from the illustrations. You will also be introduced to the habit of looking at things and thinking about what you see in terms of stitches and materials. This gradually builds up to the making of an embroidery panel.

Next comes a discussion of possible subject matter and ways in which we can begin to notice special qualities about things we have not paused to think about before.

Translating such possibilities into threads, fabrics and a method of working of course means producing a design. Learning to make your own design for embroidery is exciting and satisfying and does not depend on having special skills in drawing and painting before you start. While some people are happy to use drawing, others arrive at their designs by other means. There are a great variety of ways in which a good design can be achieved and these are described at length.

Many of the people who say 'I can't draw' or 'I am awful at art' will cut out shapes from pieces of paper or fabric and arrange them to produce patterns and designs without realising that they are virtually 'drawing' with their scissors and their fingers! So drawing is not a matter of making pencil studies in perspective – in fact these have very little use in embroidery. Think of the lively and beautiful peasant designs from many countries that we so much enjoy; these obviously do not depend on that sort of ability. However, there is much to learn about other aspects of design such as the use of line and shape, rhythm and movement, colour, etc, which are discussed in the book. Information is also given on ways of using pencils, pens, chalk and charcoal, paint, etc, in the hope that you will be inspired to experiment.

The next stage is the translation of a design into materials and this will involve the choice of a method or particular approach. The word 'stitch' covers very broad and varied areas of activity. Some people enjoy exploring the enormous range of stitches invented by people the world over, trying them out in the great variety of threads available. Others enjoy putting fabrics together and keeping their stitches invisible, as in patchwork. This book should encourage the exploration of materials and ideas, so that people learn to say as they work, not 'Is it right?' but 'Does it work?' – in other words to make their own decisions.

Inspired to Stitch is for all embroiderers who enjoy working in an individual and creative way and want to extend their scope. I hope it will also tempt some new embroiderers, especially youngsters and their teachers, and inspire those who have started off by using kits to venture along some new and exciting paths, exploring the joys of this rewarding craft.

Boy

BEGINNINGS IN CREATIVE EMBROIDERY

Chapter 1 invites you to work through a series of twelve exercises, using simple and well-known stitches for the first eight, with the addition of fabric collage in the following four, and finally to create your own embroidery panel.

These exercises all make very specific requirements of you, eg to use one thread only, one stitch only and to work in parallel lines, the only freedom being the choice of the stitch you use, the variations in its size, and the distance between the lines. Believe it or not, ten people will produce ten very different pieces of work when tackling this exercise!

You are also asked to think about the colour and texture of threads and how they relate to each other and to the background fabric.

As the chapter develops, each exercise builds on previous discoveries and you are encouraged to begin relating stitches to the things you see, eg fly stitch to grasses and twigs, cretan stitch to water in a pond, etc. Later you are asked to make simple sketches of car wheels and then to create a design from them. There is an exercise in which you design from a photograph, translating this into fabrics and stitchery and, lastly, you design a panel of your own choice. There is also help with the various technicalities and procedures as they arise, such as enlarging a design, applying fabrics, etc.

If you are a beginner in embroidery, these exercises will help you get the feel of threads and fabrics and to learn how to make stitches 'say' what you want them to. You will learn how to present your work, and produce a well-made panel.

If you are an experienced embroiderer, you may yet find a challenge in some of the exercises and perhaps extend your handling of various stitches by having to focus on fulfilling some specific demands; you may even gain inspiration from what you produce and visualise a very large piece of work emerging from an experiment on a tiny sampler!

STITCHES

There are many good books available which explain particular stitches (see Bibliography).

It is not necessary to know a great number of different stitches, although one sometimes feels the need to search for something new and exactly right for a particular situation. It is surprising and satisfying to discover how much variety can be obtained by using just a few different stitches, but varying the texture and colour of the threads and scale of the stitches. Notice too the effect of light on shiny threads as they change direction.

1 LINE AND STITCHERY

In this first exercise we begin by exploring the use of just one simple stitch in three different ways. Many people only know one or two different stitches, eg running, back or chain stitch, etc. Any of these would be suitable. Perhaps, though, you may be an experienced embroiderer, but venturing for the first

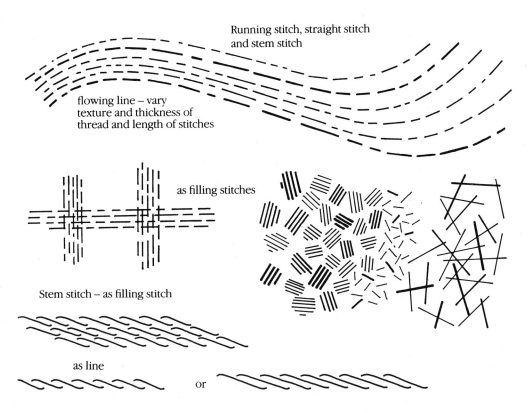

Running stitch, straight stitch and stem stitch

flowing line – vary texture and thickness of thread and length of stitches

as filling stitches

Stem stitch – as filling stitch

as line

or

time into a more free and unconventional approach; in this case you might enjoy bringing your knowledge to bear by choosing a more unusual stitch.

In the first exercise the restrictions imposed are very tight indeed – one stitch, one thread, parallel lines only! It is a challenge for you to make something interesting within the strictest limitations; one day you may find yourself referring to your sampler and applying this mode of stitching as just the right thing for some particular context. The second exercise widens the scope and you are already having to make decisions on colour, texture and choice of line, while the last exercise explores the use of the same stitch used singly to create a textured area.

It is important to position the resulting work very carefully on your fabric to produce a well–balanced sampler, which should be mounted at a later stage (see page 16).

The materials required are detailed below.

Background fabric   Suitable fabrics are hessian, crash, plain furnishing fabrics, woollen tweeds or rayon dupion, etc. It is important that fabrics are firm and soft enough to stitch through comfortably. Choose your fabric and cut a piece about 9in (23cm) square. Using a tacking thread, stitch a border of about 1in (2.5cm) on all edges of the fabric and embroider within these margins to allow for mounting.

Threads   Choose one colour range only, which looks good on your background fabric. Threads should vary in texture, thickness and colour: if you choose greens, they could be light, vivid, dark, some veering towards yellow, others towards blue, some which are rather grey and muted. Threads like tapestry and crewel wools, Sylko perlé, Anchor Soft cotton, stranded cottons, silks, oddments of knitting wools, fine sewing threads, etc, would be suitable.

Needles   Crewel or chenille needles in different sizes. These have sharp points and long eyes, so will take the thicker threads. Vary the needle size to suit the thread you are working with and avoid using very long threads, as they tangle and begin to wear as they are pulled through the fabric.

Small sharp scissors and pencil and paper

Exercises

a   Using one stitch only (eg back stitch) and one thread only (one thick enough to have impact), make a small design, about 2-2½in (5-6cm) across, in which you stitch in parallel lines, but vary the length of the stitch and the distance between the lines.

b   Use the same stitch, but this time vary the thickness and texture of your threads and the colour within the chosen range.

Notice the texture of your threads, woolly, hairy, silky, smooth, etc. With young children you could extend this into language and movement; a smooth shiny thread might be expressed in gliding movements and so on.

Lines can be straight, flowing, spiral, overlapping, etc. Think of more words that could be interesting to interpret in embroidery stitches. You may like to draw a few lines on paper first, then build up a design on the fabric based on your chosen type of line, again varying the size of your stitches. Start and finish a line with a few small running stitches, then a back stitch or two to taper the ends.

c   Once more use the same stitch, but this time singly, with stitches that vary in size, texture, colour within the range, and direction. Stitches can be placed on top of or across each other and be used densely or as a fine sprinkling.

Discussions of the work

This is a very helpful thing to do. A group of people working together could put their finished or unfinished pieces on a table, or up on the wall, and discuss them. It will at once be apparent that people work differently; some pieces will be bold and free, others delicate and some neat and meticulous. Already the different personalities are showing! Then try to work out why a certain area is so successful and why another is not.

2 A FAMILY OF STITCHES

Many stitches fit into groups, or 'families', such as feather stitch, buttonhole, cross stitch, etc. It is interesting to investigate some of these variations on a theme and, for this exercise, the chain stitch 'family' has been chosen because it offers a wealth of attractive stitches which lend themselves for use in many different situations and relate well to each other: whipped chain, cable, zigzag, knotted, chequered, detached, double, rosette, twisted, raised chain band, etc. It is a good idea to extend your knowledge of stitches by learning and practising some of them.

Materials required
A piece of background fabric as before
A variety of threads within one colour range
A stitch book
The usual tools of an embroiderer, including paper and pencil.

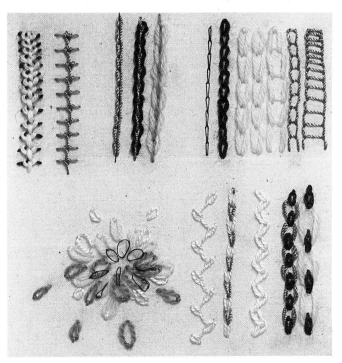

Chain stitch sampler by Gill Davis: (clockwise from top left) 2 rows of raised chain band, 3 of back-stitched chain, 4 of chain stitch, 3 of open chain stitch, 2 of threaded chain, 1 of zigzag chain, 1 of chequered chain, 1 of feathered chain, and a group of detached chain stitches

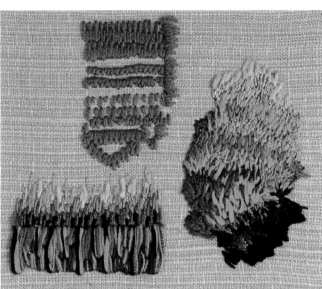

Line and stitchery examples by
Valerie Webberley (above),
Kitty Weedon (above right)
Nancy Cowcher (right)

You can teach yourself each of your chosen stitches by first trying them out on a spare scrap of material. Now practise each of them in an interesting arrangement on your background fabric, perhaps planning this first on paper. Select your threads carefully in relation to each other and consider the scale of the stitches.

In this way you will produce a sampler to which you can refer in future when looking for just the right stitch for some special use.

You might enjoy investigating other families of stitches in the same way, thereby extending your own knowledge or 'vocabulary'.

3 HERRINGBONE, CRETAN AND FLY STITCHES

There is certain similarity between herringbone, cretan and fly stitches, perhaps in their potential for evoking images from nature.

Try using these stitches freely, either individually or combining all three; the sketches show some possible ways of working which might help stimulate ideas (and note the use of fly stitches in *Rockface, Drumbeg* to describe dry grasses, page 22).

Why not look at a pond or stream, trees and bushes, plants, etc, and think whether you could depict them with these stitches? Jot down your observations and make a few notes to help you remember how things looked. Choose a background fabric of suitable colour and select your threads

10

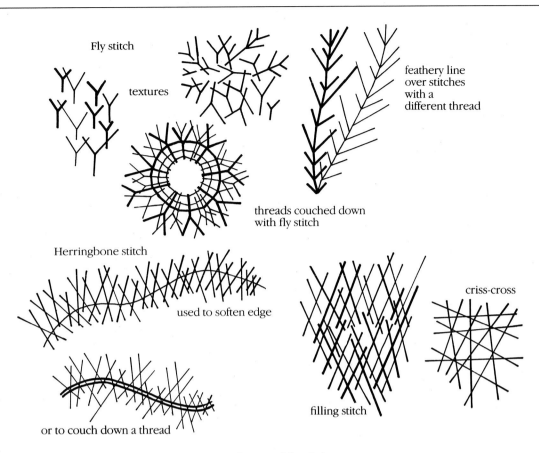

Fly stitch

textures

feathery line over stitches with a different thread

threads couched down with fly stitch

Herringbone stitch

used to soften edge

or to couch down a thread

criss-cross

filling stitch

Herringbone and fly stitches

Reeds by Christine Cooper. Great depth is created with only Cretan and fly stitches in threads of varied thickness and texture, and a limited colour range. *9¹/₂in (24cm) square*

Trees and Twigs by Gordon Faulkner

(below)
Grasses by Elizabeth Ashurst

carefully, perhaps including some fine sewing cottons among them. Have a go, and see what happens (see *Reeds* by Christine Cooper.)

For her panel *Tuscan Summer* (overleaf) Jan Attrill chose to work mainly in cretan stitch as it conveys so well the tall cypress trees which dominate the landscape in Tuscany. While on holiday she took many photographs of the country-side and buildings and loved the warm gold of the farm-houses. A photograph was the source material for a drawing prior to the actual stitching. Cream evenweave linen was used for the background and a small amount of lightly painted muslin was overlaid. Threads used were mohair, silk, perlé and stranded cotton. A small group of pink and purple French knots depict the wild cyclamen which carpeted the ground.

Another way of using these stitches is to create a border pattern that could be used in dress embroidery or on a box, a bag or a cushion, etc. Let us create a formal design using one of the variations in the herringbone stitch family, eg double, laced, threaded or tied. Work a line of even and fairly open herringbone, perhaps over a narrow ribbon, then enrich the stitches with a contrasting colour or thread and add fly stitches in something fine or silky. Repeat the line in mirror image, with both lines touching.

How would you use this on a box, in vertical or horizontal

4 COUCHING

Couching is a way of laying thickish threads, or cords, on the surface of a fabric and holding them down with a fine thread that can either be matching or contrasting.

Try this for yourself, first laying a flowing line on your material in a thick thread, and holding it in position with pins. Take the ends through to the back to be neatened later. Now begin your stitching with the fine thread, working straight across and making sure the stitches are always placed at right-angles, which is not so easy on a curve!

Lay two or three additional thick threads in the same way, alongside and touching the first one, but try making each one shorter to vary the thickness of the line and to avoid hard, abrupt looking ends. Decide whether to put your small stitches in line with each other, or to alternate them in a 'brickwork' pattern (see diagram overleaf). You can also vary the placing of these stitches, perhaps clustering them and then spreading them out, which could be fun if you are using varied colours.

It is also interesting to experiment by couching threads down with other stitches such as cretan, herringbone, fly or cross stitch, etc. Glance through your stitch book for alternative ideas. If you are working with long free stitches, it will be necessary to place them so that the couched thread cannot move about (see diagram).

Can you think of something you have seen that would be interesting to carry out in one of these ways? Some of the semi-precious stones might offer possibilities, such as the polished surface of a piece of malachite, with its decorative rings of pale greens and blacks on a rich green background – or what about a snake or a furry caterpillar? Perhaps an idea for a panel will emerge from one of your samplers.

Textured, knobbly, or uneven threads intended for knitting or weaving can be an interesting addition to the conventional range of embroidery threads. They will also need to be couched on the surface, using a fine thread in matching colour, as they would probably break if you tried to stitch with them.

lines? Could you work it in circular form for the lid? If you decide to use it as a border design on a cushion, the corners will present a problem which can be resolved by using a small mirror placed at 45° across the border. You will then see how it can be worked and where it will be best to cut across the design. An exercise in problem-solving for you!

For further suggestions on pattern-making, see Chapter 5.

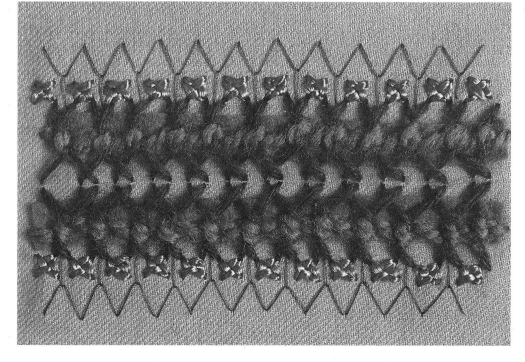

(above) Cretan and herringbone stitch with French knots

Border Pattern – herringbone, sorbello and fly stitches with ribbons

Tuscan Summer by Jan Attrill, using mainly Cretan stitch and some French knots.
13 x 10¹/₂in (33 x 27cm)

Medusa by Kitty Weedon, an example of couching.
16 x 21in (41 x 53cm)

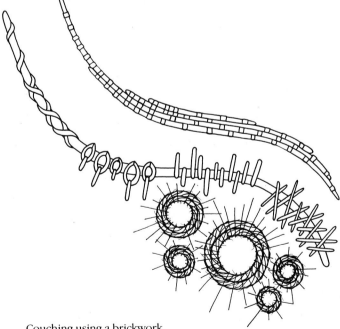

Couching using a brickwork pattern (top) and a variety of stitches (below)

Kitty Weedon says that it was finding a hank of hand spun and dyed wool that started her on her panel, *Medusa*.

The wool, with its uneven texture and varying shades of mustard yellow, seemed to wriggle between my fingers and *Medusa* took over.

As there was only a small quantity of wool, I first laid a background of orange curtain material with two layers of yellow net to give depth. The face was intended to be mask-like with the transparent complexion that often accompanies auburn hair and was made of a sandwich of pale pink silk with dacron padding between. The only strong feature being the cold, green eyes worked in stranded cotton in blanket stitch. The completed face was appliquéd to the background of the hair and then I was able to mound the hand spun wool over and round the face – couching it in place at very infrequent intervals where another strand of wool crossed over it. The curl in the wool dictated where it should go – it was more in control of the final placing than I was.

The snakes emerging from the hair were made from chair braid joined edge to edge to form a flattened tube.

MOUNTING A FINISHED PIECE

By now you will have accumulated quite a number of finished samplers. It is most important that these should be well mounted and treasured, so now is the time to do this. (For a more detailed discussion of presentation see Chapter 7.)

Finished work is often crumpled and puckered, but on no account attempt to press it, as this could flatten the textures you have so carefully created. It will need to be stretched and mounted, and the transformation that takes place is quite amazing!

Stretching

Lay several layers of newsprint or blotting paper on a drawing-board, or piece of wood that will accept drawing-pins (thumb tacks) and sprinkle them with water. Alternatively use an old tea-towel dipped in water, wrung out and spread smoothly across the board. Place your embroidery face-upwards in the middle of the board and pin it out from the centre top, stretching gently to the centre bottom and then from side to side until it is evenly stretched, straight and square, and leave it overnight to dry.

Cutting a window-mount

Find a piece of card of suitable colour and decide on the size of the window-mount which will display your work to its greatest advantage. To do this, cut four long strips of paper and lay one along each side of the embroidery to frame it.

Move them about until you are satisfied with the arrangement, then mark the area with pins and measure it carefully.

Next, decide how wide you want the margins to be, allowing equal widths at the top and the sides and a little more at the bottom. Alternatively, the top need not be the same as the sides, especially if you decide to work with a standard size of mount, but the base is traditionally deeper, so the design or picture does not seem to be slipping downwards out of its frame. Notice the page layout in any book, magazine, newspaper, etc. Draw the shape of the mount and the 'window' on the right side of the card, using a T-square or a set square and a sharp pencil to ensure accuracy.

Using a craft knife with a sharp blade and a steel ruler, cut out the shape, then cut out the window, remembering to protect the table you are working on with card, or a piece of hardboard. Place your steel ruler over the mount so that, if the knife should slip, it will cut into the centre part of the mount which is to be discarded. Dig the point of the knife in at the corner where you start, cut steadily, and dig it in at the next corner to act as a brake. Keep on cutting until the card comes away clean.

Stick a piece of Sellotape (Scotchtape) face upwards across the underside of two opposite corners of the fabric, then lay the mount on top, placing it very carefully, noting the straight grain of the fabric. Press it down firmly over the taped corners to fix it in place, then turn it over and tape all the edges in position; get help with this as the fabric needs to be quite taut. Neaten the back with sugar or cartridge paper, using an

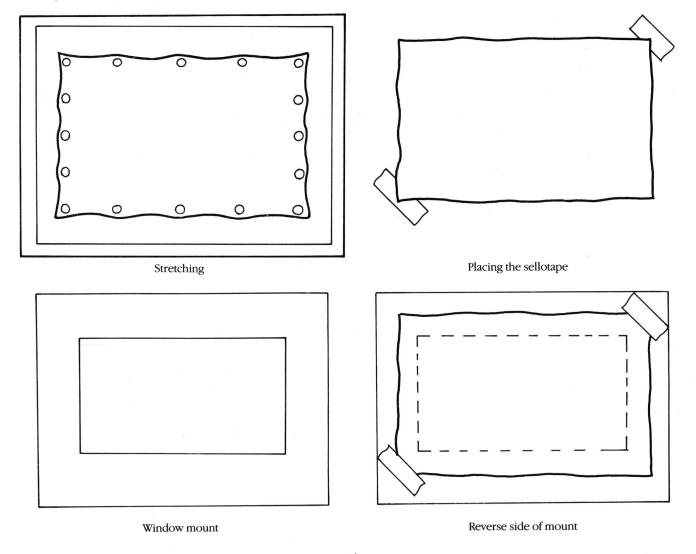

Stretching

Placing the sellotape

Window mount

Reverse side of mount

adhesive or double-sided tape to keep it in place.

On the back write a brief description of the exercise so that, in years to come, you will remember what it was about.

There are a number of reasons for taking trouble to preserve your work in this way: firstly, it provides impetus to complete and record each exercise and, secondly, you will have this reference material for your future work. If you are a teacher, or thinking of becoming one some day, you will have some invaluable visual aids. Many people take City and Guilds examinations and find that this may lead to a new career in teaching.

Unfortunately card is very expensive but it is sometimes possible to persuade a picture-framer to sell you the off-cuts more cheaply. Another possibility is to keep some of the exercises unmounted in a plastic sleeve of the type designed to fit into a file, with the exercise written up in detail on a facing sheet of paper, and perhaps including a sheet with jotted down ideas following the exercise that might lead to something in the future.

A larger piece of work will need different treatment (see Chapter 7).

5 STRAIGHT STITCHES, SATIN STITCH BLOCKS AND SEEDING

Sometimes the simplest of all stitches can be quite telling when used in a lively and imaginative way. Let us look back at the very first exercise of the Course, in which one simple stitch was used in parallel lines, varying the length of stitch and distance between the rows. This idea can now be built on if we use lines, or broken lines of running stitch and occasional back stitches, quite freely.

Think for a little while about the subject 'Bright lights over the dark water'. At some time you may have looked across a bay and seen lamps by the sea-shore reflected in the sea and perhaps a few dark silhouettes of boats; or maybe you have looked down the river towards a bridge that is lit up at night. What sort of shapes do the shadows and reflections make?

The aim is to evoke the image just by using this economical mode of stitching. The choice of background fabric will be important, as will the threads of various thickness that work successfully on it. Shiny threads can add to the feeling of life and sparkle in your picture, probably with the thicker threads in the foreground and quite fine ones in the distance and for the sky. Keep the piece fairly small; you may find it easier to keep it taut on a frame. (See page 34 on using a frame.)

The next exercise is to work with blocks of satin stitch in various white threads on a white background, to evoke a suggestion of buildings in a city. You might be looking across from the other side of a river, or from a bridge or the top of a high building. The blocks will consist of rows of satin stitch producing either vertical or horizontal rectangles, and perhaps a few obliques at 45° if that will help your design.

Again, keep the work quite small, with the fabric held taut on a frame, varying the kinds and thicknesses of the threads to include both matt and shiny. Vary the sizes of the blocks, from about 1½in (4cm) as your largest dimension, to some really tiny ones in fine threads or silks. When working with satin stitch it is a good idea to use a fine fabric with a clear grain-line, such as grosgrain, to help keep the stitches straight. You will no doubt discover that there are many versions of white!

In the third exercise we shall explore the way that shiny threads such as silks and perlés will catch the light when

White on White – satin stitch blocks

New Embroidery Group cover showing satin stitch blocks drawn by Molly Picken

stitched in different directions and produce a seeming change of colour. Do a small sampler based on satin stitch blocks, again using a smooth fabric with a clear grain line and mounted to keep it taut. Work a number of blocks, using just one type of thread and varying the stitch direction to include verticals, horizontals and 45° obliques.

Another variation is to use stitches not so much in blocks, but grouped together in a much more random way, not necessarily touching or parallel with each other. Working in this way you might create an image of rocks, the bark of a tree, long grass, corn, etc, especially if the scale varies and if the types of thread vary to include wools and thicker threads along with the finer ones.

Seeding is the use of tiny, fine and individual straight stitches placed freely in various directions to produce an even texture, or one that thins out from a concentrated area. It can be worked in just one thread or in several different ones. The same applies to the colour and the length of the stitches.

It is easy to visualise the combination of seeding and the use of free satin stitch blocks, especially the more random variety.

The two panels of butterflies by Muriel Best present interesting examples of the use of satin stitch blocks. She was inspired by the pattern, shape and colour to be found in the different species of moths and butterflies:

> Even the humblest brown moth seen in close-up shows a variety of markings and colour tones. A microscopic view of the wings of these insects reveals that they are constructed of hundreds of tiny scales all slotting together to give pattern and changing colour which alters according to the direction and reflection of light.

It is this aspect that is translated into embroidery using small satin stitches in blocks of varying colour to create the illusion of the scales. Fine silk threads are used for the stitchery and the background fabric is also silk.

Audrey Welch's *Seascape* is an example of straight stitches being used to create a feeling of great power and movement.

Seascape by Audrey Welch, using straight stitches (detail)

Green Silver Line and **The Purple Edged Copper** by Muriel Best, who uses tiny satin-stitch blocks in silk. Each is *6½ x 9in (16 x 23cm)*

6 'SPOT' STITCHES

French knots, spiders' webs and woven wheels are all individual stitches, complete in themselves, but which can be used together most successfully.

French knots
First learn to do a French knot, then try varying the texture and thickness of the thread. The books tell you to take the thread twice around the needle, but it can be taken once or three times round – why not experiment? French knots can be packed very tightly together, with others worked on top, and then thinned outwards, smoothly and gradually, perhaps using a thinner thread or wrapping only once round the needle. Another way is to scatter them carefully in twos and threes in a seemingly random fashion.

French knots have been used in both these ways in the panel *Rockface, Drumbeg* (page 22). An outcrop of rock in Scotland inspired this design: the slanting seams with their broken surfaces, the contrasts of light and dark, the secondary rhythms created by the growth of the lichen and also the stony and scrubby path at the base.

The background fabric is dark brown, built up with a 'jigsaw puzzle' of layers of corduroy and felt. Next I tore pieces of black, yellow and orange net and arranged them to give variation in colour and tone, and to enhance the feeling of movement. Straight stitches were embroidered both underneath and on top of the net. French knots seemed just right for the lichen, and these were built up very densely, varying in size and colour and then fading out gradually in various directions. Fly stitch was used for the foreground twigs and reeds.

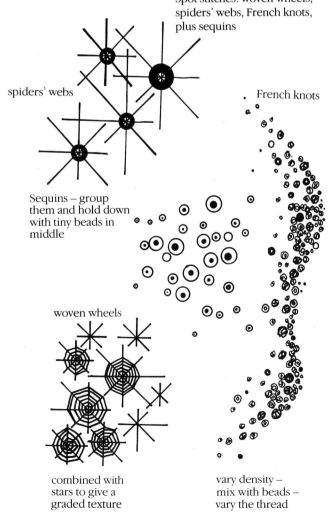

Spot stitches: woven wheels, spiders' webs, French knots, plus sequins

spiders' webs

French knots

Sequins – group them and hold down with tiny beads in middle

woven wheels

combined with stars to give a graded texture

vary density – mix with beads – vary the thread

Spiders' webs and woven wheels

Spiders' webs and woven wheels are fascinating: so simple that quite young children can do them, and yet so effective. They are based on the spokes of a wheel, usually eight for the spiders' webs and an odd number for the woven wheels.

Spiders' webs are woven using a blunt-ended tapestry needle, with a continuous line of back stitch starting at the centre and working round, either to produce a small worked central circle, or stitched solidly to the outer edges. The colour of the thread can be changed several times if you wish, or the same one used throughout.

Another interesting thing to do is to stand a large bead with a fairly big hole on the fabric. Come up through the central hole to work the spokes using a strong, but not too thick, thread and then to stitch round quite solidly, probably using a thicker thread. This raises the surface to give a three dimensional quality; at one time wooden button-moulds could be used, but these are unobtainable now.

Long threads can be carried out from the centre of a woven wheel raised in this way, then three or four tiny beads threaded on each spoke and back stitched through the last one to hold them in just the right place, before the threads are taken down through the fabric. The effect is very much like the long strands of a cobweb, especially if fine silken threads are used.

Instead of using a back stitch round the spokes of the wheel, ie under two stitches and back over one, try the reverse – over two and back under one. This produces a smooth flat result which contrasts with the rib effect pro-

duced by the back stitch. This type looks best when the stitching is carried right to the ends of the spokes.

The truly woven wheel must be carried out over an uneven number of spokes. Start in the middle and work over one and under one until you have worked a circle in the centre, or completely covered the spokes.

Finally, instead of working the eight spokes from the centre outwards, work from top to bottom, side to side, then the diagonals, and put a neat stitch in the middle to hold them all in place and leave it at that, like a star.

Experiment using some or all of these suggestions, then work a sampler in a limited colour range incorporating all the wheels and perhaps French knots as well. It does seem rather hard to work a beautiful stitch and then partially cover it up, but do try putting three woven wheels close together, then a fourth one in the middle and on top!

7 TRANSLATING MARK-MAKING INTO STITCHERY

Another approach to stitchery is through simple mark-making. Many people would not think of picking up a paintbrush once they have left school, except perhaps to encourage children, as parents or teachers. Mark-making however, is not at all demanding.

You will need black poster paint and a fairly thick brush, an old plate as a palette, water, paper, a rag and some newspaper on the table. Use cheap paper so it will not feel too wasteful if it all ends up in the bin!

(left) **Woven Wheels**

(above) Mark-making into fabrics by Kitty Weedon

Mark-making by Kitty Weedon

Dip your brush into water and then into the paint, and stir some of the paint on the plate, diluting it a little if necessary, but keeping it fairly thick.

Now try making various brush marks on the paper just by letting the point flow across in different ways. Then try pressing the brush down flat and keep repeating this kind of mark first densely, then thinning out, lying in different directions, overlapping etc, to cover an area about 3-4in (8-10cm) across. Try painting a scrap of frayed hessian, or some screwed up paper and press these down several times close together. Paint the flat end of a pencil or the edge of a ruler and print from them, or from the edge of a folded piece of cardboard. A piece of string dipped in the paint and swirled round like a compass can produce some lovely marks! Even people with plenty of experience can discover new textures that they might also enjoy including in a more traditional type of painting.

Now examine what you have done, and select a small area that looks interesting and that suggests the possibility of stitchery. By now you know how to use quite a lot of different stitches and here is an opportunity to combine several of them in the translation of the mark-making into embroidery. You may prefer just to produce another small sampler, but if a rather special piece of pattern has emerged why not carry it out on a slightly larger scale? As usual you will be considering what type of colours to use, and the texture and thickness of threads, as you tackle this exercise.

There is a further section on mark-making in Chapter 2, page 60.

8 THE USE OF COLOUR

It is useful to learn something about colour theory; if you are having problems in putting colours together, or trying to pep up a piece of work that does not quite come to life, it is handy to turn to the theory for some suggestions. This area is examined in greater depth in Chapter 5, but just now it will suffice to take a look at the colours and then follow this up with a practical exercise.

The colour circle

The three *primary* colours are yellow, red and blue. The three *secondary* colours are a mixture of the primary colours:

Yellow + red = orange
Red + blue = purple
Blue + yellow = green

The colours opposite each other in the colour circle are called *complementary* colours:

Yellow and purple
Red and green
Blue and orange

A voided shape

This exercise is a practical exploration of the theory you have just read about. What really happens when you work with yellow and purple, or red and green, or blue and orange? Take a look at the examples on page 26 and then shut the book and produce your own solution to the problem.

Materials required

Background fabric A background fabric about 8-9in (20-23cm) square in white or black.

Threads A variety of threads in two complementary colours, eg a really wide range of yellows and purples, light, brilliant and dark, with warm orangey or cold yellowy ones and purples including violet and plum colours, plus some which are rather dull and muted.

On your background fabric mark out a simple shape such as a circle, square, rectangle or egg shape, about 2in (5cm) across, not bigger or it will take a long time to work. Mark the shape by tacking a line, or using a white crayon (those made specially for quilters are ideal), or drawing a fine line with a hard pencil (which will disappear eventually). Choose a 'spot' stitch, which could be an isolated chain stitch from your samplers, a fly stitch, woven wheels and stars of various kinds, or French knots, etc. The aim is to stitch on the outside of your shape, leaving the centre voided, using yellows on one side and purples on the other. It will not be necessary to touch the line everywhere as the eye will 'close' the gaps and the shape will still be clear. Think of fallen leaves blown up against a wall and densely packed, but thinning out so they gradually fine away towards the edge of your fabric, and remember to leave about 1in (2.5cm) round the edges for mounting.

The problem to be resolved is how to make a smooth transition from the yellow to the purple. You could perhaps dot the purples into the yellows and vice versa, where they meet, or drain the colour out gradually so that you are working in muted colours and greys and creams, or you could travel round the colour circle, from yellow to orange and through red to purple, or perhaps the other way through green and blue, or you could combine these ideas – it is up to you!

When you have finished, pin up your work, stand back and make a critical assessment of it. Ask yourself 'What was I trying to do and have I been successful?' If not, then perhaps cutting a few stitches out or adding more might make all the difference.

Four examples of this exercise are illustrated. See also Margaret Bailey's panel, *Poppies* (page 31), which uses many reds and greens with striking effect.

The embroiderer worked from her own photograph of a poppyfield in the Chilterns, first enlarging her design and colouring it with crayons. The picture was built up on a Wedgwood green background, using green and red textured fabrics and torn net for sky, clouds and trees. These, the distant poppies and some of the stalks were machined freely. The poppies were made of masses of heart-shaped pieces, machined and straight-stitched on vertical lines. Nearer stalks were worked in stem stitch and couching.

9 EXPLORING FABRIC COLLAGE

So far we have focussed on stitchery and will now examine some of the possibilities offered in the use of applied fabrics. In tackling the stitch exercises we shall have come to recognise and enjoy the qualities of the varied threads we have been using, and so will be ready to consider the look and the feel of fabrics in a similar way.

Collect together all the oddments of plain fabrics you can lay hands on, such as silk, wool of different types, cottons, corduroys, velvets, dress and furnishing fabrics and some

Rockface, Drumbeg using French knots, straight and fly stitches. *15 x 10¹/₂in (38 x 27cm)*

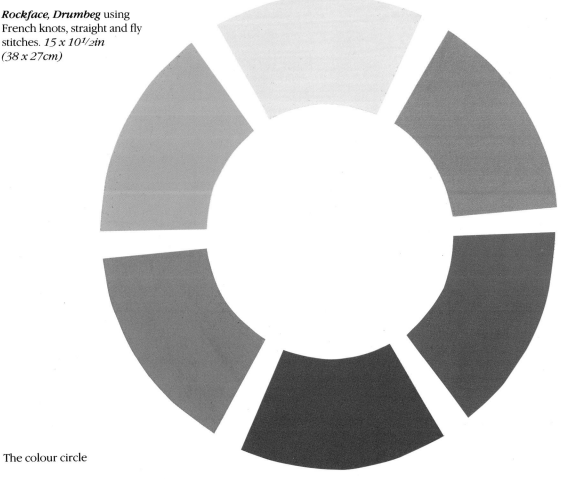

The colour circle

transparent materials such as net, chiffon, organza, nylon tights (panty hose), etc. Try begging from your friends and neighbours, searching through remnant bins, visiting market stalls, charity shops, etc, and cutting up your old clothes! It is a good idea to sort them all into colours and store them in separate bags.

For this first exercise choose just one colour range, preferably the one in which you have the greatest variety of colours and textures. Suppose you have chosen blue: select the most intense middle blue for your centre of interest and any fabrics ranging through turquoise to green, blue to purple. Pick out both the lighter and darker versions of all these colours and also some greyish and muted ones.

Use a piece of white cotton as a background: a piece of old sheeting would do, as it will be completely covered by the fabrics. It should be about 14 x 16in (36 x 41cm) to allow a 2in (5cm) border on all sides for mounting.

The aim is to build up a collage of rectangles of various sizes and shapes, cut from your different fabrics and arranged in a pleasing manner on the background, with the most intense colour as a centre of interest or focal point.

First press your materials, including the background, then cut out the rectangles, keeping the edges along the true grain of each fabric. If this is not easy to see draw out a thread, either from the warp or the weft and near the edge, then cut along the line thus produced.

Now position your focal point and main feature in the design. It could be central, but would probably be better placed a little to one side and either slightly up or down, or perhaps near a corner. Arrange the other fabrics around it, keeping them parallel to the edges of the fabric, with a strong vertical and horizontal emphasis, allowing a small underlap with every fabric to avoid irritating gaps; pin them in place.

Move the pieces about, perhaps cutting some smaller, or recutting some larger ones. There are many aspects to consider, such as colour relationships – whether to separate the greeny blues from the mauvey ones or to enjoy mixing them; where to place the darker tones and also how to place a heavy fabric, especially if it is also dark or strong in colour.

It sounds like child's play, but it is really quite an absorbing and difficult exercise!

When you feel satisfied with your arrangement, having looked at it near to and then stood back to check it, the next stage is to stitch all the fabrics on to the background. Do this either by hand, using a small stab stitch on the top and a big stitch at the back, and using a matching thread, or with a zig-zag stitch on the sewing machine. If that is not available, a straight stitch on the machine will do very well. Do not worry too much about matching every colour as long as the tone is right.

Adhesives are unsuitable, in that they are likely to come through and go yellow in time, and are also hard and unpleasant to stitch through, but you could use Bondaweb (fusible webbing), an adhesive material, between the two layers of fabric and iron them in place. Do not be tempted to hold down your fabrics by using a decorative stitch, eg buttonhole or herringbone, as this could give a hard, insistent effect. Put your decorative stitches where you choose, not where you need!

Now you are ready to enrich your fabric collage with stitchery, bearing in mind the vertical and horizontal aspect of the design. Which stitches will you choose? Will you put emphasis on line stitches, or perhaps cover small areas with blocks of raised chain band in two or more colours? Will you use some satin stitch blocks rather freely, or emphasise groups of colour with couched lines, etc? How will you emphasise your focal point? Perhaps bullion knots would be just the right thing? If so, look them up in your stitch book, and practise them first in the usual way. Another problem is knowing when to stop – something we all face from time to time!

10 FABRICS AND STITCHERY – SOFTENING EDGES

In this exercise we shall be designing a small panel, by arranging a few simple shapes on a background and learning how to integrate them by softening the edges.

Materials required

Fabrics Plain fabrics in one colour range only, but varying in texture, such as silk, woollen tweed, synthetics, velvet, etc, and some scraps of net in dark and bright colours. A background fabric, about 9½in (24cm) across, that harmonises with them.

Threads A variety of threads in the same colour range and a few in a contrasting colour. A range of threads suitable for the sewing-machine.

Choose some simple example of natural form with an interesting silhouette shape, such as a leaf, an apple, a shell, toadstool, etc. Select a good example and draw it carefully, or look for a photograph or factual drawing in a book.

Draw the same shape three times in different sizes, then cut them out and use them as pattern shapes for cutting your fabrics. Now select three fabrics, varying in colour and texture, that look well together on the background. Give careful thought as to which fabric will be the most dominant; will it be the dark velvet, the vivid silk or the pale woolly one? Does this relationship change when they are laid on the background? It might be wise to avoid having the largest shape in the most powerful tone or colour.

The arrangement is important. Will you overlap the shapes at all or keep them separate? Try to place them so that the spaces around and between them look nicely balanced. Normally we should try to keep the grain-lines of the fabric true to that of the background, but in this case other aspects are more important.

When you are happy with the placing, pin or tack them in position, then stitch them down either by hand or by using Bondaweb (fusible webbing), or with the sewing-machine. If you are using a zigzag, a fairly close stitch will negotiate any complicated shapes more easily than a wide one.

Now lay different colours of net across the shapes, or two pieces, slightly shifted. It is always surprising how, for instance, a vivid red will make only soft and gentle variations to a colour. Experiment with lots of colours and, when you have chosen the best two or three, cut them out using your paper patterns. Net usually looks most effective when moved so that it lies partly on and partly off a shape. However, before you fix it in place, decide if you wish to do some further work with the sewing-machine.

It is interesting to 'draw' round some of the shapes quite freely with the sewing machine, or to use the lines to help link the shapes together and to integrate them into the background. Do this with a straight stitch on the machine and

Exploring fabric collage by
Valerie Webberley

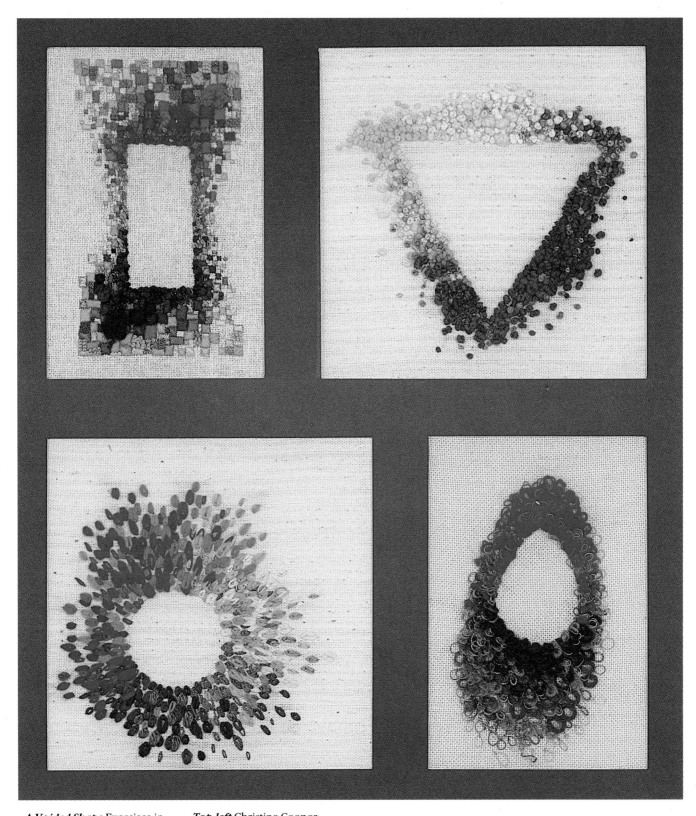

A Voided Shape Exercises in working with complementary colours

Top left Christine Cooper – satin stitch blocks and French knots, *5 x 8¹/₂in (13 x 22cm)*
Top right Kitty Weedon – French knots, *8¹/₂ (22cm) square*
Bottom left Margaret Bailey – chain stitch, *8¹/₂in (22cm) square*
Bottom right Jane Sharp – looped chain stitch, *5¹/₂ x 8¹/₂in (14 x 22cm)*

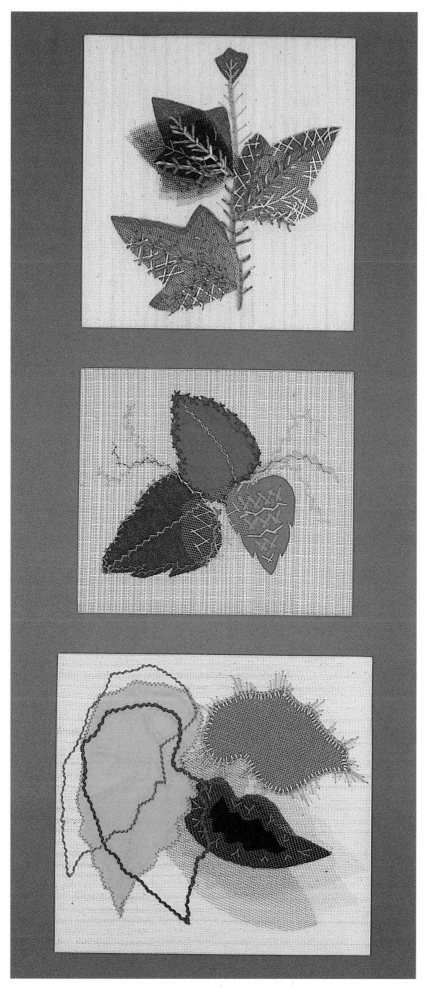

Leaves, an exercise in using
fabrics and stitchery
Top Margaret Bailey *8 x 8¹/₂in
(20 x 22cm)*
Centre Jean Knapp *8 x 7in
(20 x 18cm)*
Bottom Kitty Weedon
9 x 8¹/₂in (23 x 22cm)

the foot in place as usual. Choose appropriate colours and allow the lines to flow, perhaps close in places and swinging round more widely in others. You might practise this first, drawing your shapes in pencil on a spare piece of fabric.

When this stage is completed, position the net quite carefully and stab-stitch it in place using a thread that will not show.

The next stage is to enrich the design with carefully chosen stitches. Herringbone or cretan worked with very fine threads might help further in softening edges, or tiny scattered French knots or seeding, etc; by now you have gained quite a lot of experience in the use of stitches and will be quite able to decide for yourself. You might enjoy adding a few beads and sequins though! Three examples of this exercise are shown on page 27.

11 DESIGNING FROM CAR WHEELS

This exercise involves working from subject matter that is both man-made and geometric in form. It will build on the skills you have already acquired during the course, plus the introduction of some padding and the use of analogous colours.

Go out with pencil and paper and have a look at some car wheels, jotting down each pattern, counting the number of units used (five or eight segments, etc), noticing the proportions of the different rings and drawing an outer circle to represent the tyre.

In the previous exercise we built up a design with related shapes arranged on a background by the 'hands-on' method, ie, moving the pieces around to find how best to place them. We shall be working in a similar manner, but this time there are many more decisions to be made.

Cut paper designs for *Car Wheels* by Margaret Bailey

28

First of all, what size should the panel be? As the wheel designs are quite elaborate, and certain parts are to be padded, it would make sense to work on a much larger scale than previously. The actual size is often dictated by the size of background fabric chosen and the shape will relate to the placing of the units. It is wise to use backing material, such as a piece of calico or old sheeting, to add strength to the background. Tear this to size and tack both fabrics together.

Now cut out a number of circles of likely size using newspapers, paper bags, etc, and draw the circle for the wheel trim on each.

At this stage we need to begin visualising the actual embroidery; we can now forget about car tyres and wheel covers and begin to think about fabrics, about colour and where to use padding.

The colour must relate to your background fabric. Use analogous colour, that is, a group of colours adjacent to each other in the colour circle, such as orange, red and purple or yellow, green and blue, etc, with all their variations.

Regarding the fabrics, you could work with a variety of textures and thicknesses as before, or you might enjoy using silks, satins, taffetas, with nets and sheer fabrics such as organzas, and metallic-looking dress materials, if such are available to you.

The padding can be achieved in one of two ways. A simple shape like a circle can be raised using three circles of felt, one almost full-size, one a little smaller, and the third smaller again. The smallest piece is put down first and held in position with a few stitches; the needle is brought up near the outside of the felt and taken down again just within the edge. The next is laid on top and stitched down, then the third piece, and finally the fabric is tacked in position and stitched down with the sewing-machine.

The other method that can be used is trapunto quilting, which is described on page 131.

Now we can get down to the job of designing with the paper circles on the background fabric, hopefully with a clearer idea of how it might work out. You will need to think where you will place the various patterns, which one will become the centre of interest, how large it should be, etc. The outside parts of the circles (the tyres) could overlap each other, but the centres should be left to display the patterns. You will gradually come to your own conclusions, and decide how many units you will use – it does not have to be six! Pin down the papers and tack round each circle; make a note of which is which, perhaps by numbering them.

Select your fabrics and use the papers as pattern pieces by cutting out the smaller circles as well. You can either lay the fabric pieces on top of each other or extract the centre pieces, but do remember to leave an underlap; try also to keep the grain-lines true to the background. Stitch down all the fabrics in the usual way and do the padding.

Which stitches will you use? Will you do some 'drawing' with the sewing-machine? Wheels spin; can you create this kind of effect with your stitchery?

Keep your designs. One day you might like to make use of them again for a quilted cushion, or a bed cover!

This exercise was carried out as a project by a small group of Surrey teachers. The panel by Jean Knapp and a waistcoat by Margaret Bailey (overleaf) show two very different results (see also Margaret's cut-paper designs).

The waistcoat was cut from a soft woollen fabric, darts and shoulder seams machined, then many different sized circles in black, silver, white and pink, were cut out using a variety of textures. These were placed on one front, making a heavier impact at the lower edge and becoming lighter towards the shoulder. They were balanced with smaller lighter circles on the other shoulder, continuing on to the back. After pinning, most were zigzagged by machine and decorated with hand stitchery and beads. It was finished with a black lining, silver buttons and fabric loops.

12 WORKING FROM A PHOTOGRAPH OF A LANDSCAPE

The next exercise is to design a piece of work from a photograph, preferably one you have taken yourself.

Working from a photograph is quite difficult as there is always so much more in the picture than we would want to use. It will require considerable simplification and selection of where to put emphasis and of what should be totally excluded.

It can be helpful to take a tracing of the picture, selecting only the most important aspects. This tracing can then be enlarged to get the size of design you want, while retaining the correct proportions (see the section on enlarging, below).

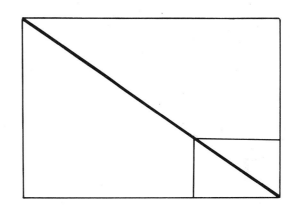

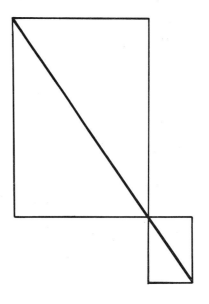

Enlarging in correct proportion

Car Wheels by Jean Knapp
16 x 12in (41 x 30cm)
Both these designs result from
the exercise 'Designing from
car wheels'

Wheels Waistcoat by Margaret
Bailey

If you carry out the design in fabric collage and stitchery we can work through a series of necessary procedures that will provide you with a breadth of technical knowledge for future projects.

The panel *Silent Forest* (overleaf) is an example of working in this way. During a holiday in Scotland we came across a forest of pine trees, many of which were dying. It was silent and eerie, and no birds were singing. I took several photographs and later designed the embroideries *Silent Forest* and *Scottish Pine-Trees* (see back cover), to express how that strange, sad area of woodland felt.

Both panels are built up in layers of fabrics, such as rayon dupion, chiffon and net, and cut away to reveal the background material, a cream-coloured silk noile, for some of the tree-trunks. Successive layers were stitched freely on the sewing-machine and holes hacked into the thinner fabrics to create an impression of the foliage and express the silent, eery quality experienced in the forest. Hand embroidery was also added on *Silent Forest*.

Enlarging
It is important to enlarge the design in correct proportion as shown in the diagram.

Next, make a grid on both the tracing and the drawing paper. Instead of using arithmetic, take a strip of paper, place it across the width of the tracing and mark points *a* and *e* on the outside edges. Fold it in half to find point *c*, and in half again for *b* and *d*, then mark these along the top and bottom of the tracing and draw lines to join them. Do this again to divide the height and repeat the process to make a grid on the drawing paper. It is important to be accurate.

Poppies by Margaret Bailey, who has used the complementary colours red and green. *23 x 15¹/₂in (58 x 39cm)*

31

Now copy the lines of your design, rectangle by rectangle on the enlarged grid, deciding whether a line cuts the edge of the rectangle half way down, or a third of the way, etc. It is not difficult and does ensure a reasonably accurate enlargement.

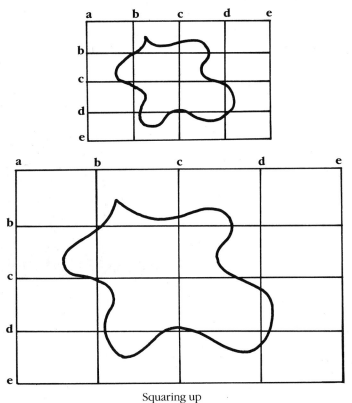

Squaring up

Transferring the design

In preparation for applying fabrics, make two tracings of the design using a ball-point pen, as tacking through pencil lines could dirty the fabrics. One tracing is for transferring the design to the background fabric, which in this case will be calico or cotton sheeting, etc, and the other for cutting up the pattern pieces.

Pin a tracing carefully in position, making sure it coincides correctly with the grain line of the fabric. Tack along the lines of the tracing through both paper and fabric, using knots on the surface so the threads can be easily removed later; make big stitches on the top and small ones on the back. Sometimes stitches can be 2-3in long (5-8cm) where a line just needs to be indicated, but should be quite fine for a detailed piece of drawing. Finally run the point of your needle through the tracing paper along the stitched lines, and lift it away.

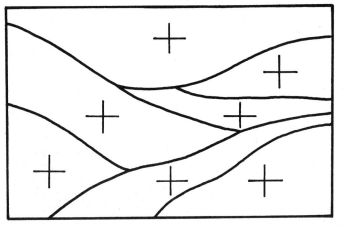

Preparing the second tracing

Cutting up the second tracing

First mark every area with a vertical and horizontal line as shown in the diagram. When the tracing is cut up, it is then quite easy to place every piece accurately on the straight grain of the fabric, so there will be no pulling or puckering when the fabrics are applied to the background. This is very important. It is sometimes useful to number your pieces if there are many of them, or if some are similar in shape, to avoid confusion.

Cutting out the fabric pieces

Collect together all the fabrics you might possibly use, then make a selection of the most likely ones and press them before you begin. Start with the ones you are most sure of and pin the paper patterns in place. Where two pieces of fabric will join, leave a small underlap on one of them so there will be no awkward gaps, but otherwise cut without leaving turnings. Pin the fabric pieces in position on the background, placing pins at right angles to the edge so you can machine across the points of the pins without tacking except where really essential. Pin your work up and see if it looks right; this is the time to make adjustments if necessary.

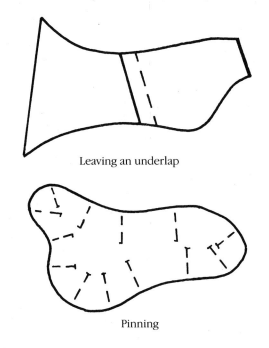

Leaving an underlap

Pinning

Attaching fabrics with the sewing-machine

Although you may be planning to use some transparent fabrics, it is probably best to machine stitch the rest of the fabrics at this stage. If you have a sewing-machine that only does a straight stitch, use this and do not worry about raw edges, or attempt to turn them under in a free piece of embroidery. Some people enjoy the rough edges and fray them more, while others prefer to keep them as neat as possible. A zigzag on a sewing-machine, especially when used on a slow speed, is ideal for giving a firm edge round your fabrics and with a matching thread will hardly show at all. It is not necessary to

Silent Forest, an example of 'Working from a Photograph of a Landscape'. *14 x 20½in (36 x 52cm)*

Tonal drawing – one tone only

Tonal drawing – several tones

change the thread to match every fabric; if the tone is right it will probably blend in quite well.

At this stage build up any additional machining you wish to do, if that seems appropriate.

The use of transparent fabrics

We have already made use of net and perhaps some other transparent fabrics, and have discovered what interesting and subtle changes can be achieved when they are superimposed on each other, or on other materials. Net can also be torn as an alternative to cutting, which can help to avoid hard edges.

If you are applying fabrics which slip or stretch like chiffon or old tights (panty hose), it may help to tack down a larger piece of fabric and machine round the shape, then cut away the edges afterwards. Net, however, is probably best applied by hand using the small stab stitches mentioned before, unless you actually want the effect of a machined line.

Stiffening fabrics

Fabrics may be stiffened with iron-on Vilene (fusible interfacing) etc. This can be helpful if they fray easily, but could change the character of something very delicate. Another possibility is to dip the fine material into a solution of PVA diluted with water and press it when dry.

To continue the embroidery design

Let us return to the point where you had taken a simplified tracing of the photograph. Now put your tracing down on a piece of drawing paper by first working across the back of the tracing with a soft B pencil, then drawing over the lines using a well-sharpened hard H pencil.

On this small outline drawing, and again using your re-sharpened B pencil, work up some solid flat areas of the darkest tones in the picture, making them as dark as you can, then produce a middle grey and finally a pale grey, leaving some places white as well. (Many thanks to Richard Box for this good idea!)

Next, enlarge your design to the required size in the manner described, taking two tracings from it. Use one for transferring the design on to the background fabric and prepare the second one for cutting up.

Collect together all likely fabrics and press them, then sort them into colours, arrange each colour into a sequence of graded tones and begin to place them as seems most appropriate, remembering that getting the tone right is more impor-

tant at this stage than getting the colour right. It can be difficult to decide whether a rather drab green is lighter or darker than the brilliant one; lay them side-by-side and half close your eyes, then try to make your own decision – indeed they may be equal in tone and so probably best kept apart.

Gradually cover the background with the fabrics (true to the grain and with underlap allowed) and pin them in position. Put your work on the wall, or pin it on the curtain with the photograph beside it, stand back and give it a critical examination. You may have to make one or two adjustments but, when you feel it looks right, machine all the pieces in place.

Pin it up again and consider how best to proceed. You may decide to add small pieces of fabric quite freely, perhaps fraying the edges, or to tear pieces of net or snip scraps of chiffon, etc, and fray these edges too. Felt might be appropriate where hard edges are required. Play around with these possibilities and then stab-stitch the bits in place.

The final stage is to consider how stitchery can be sensitively added to enhance the particular quality of the image you are creating. Build it up gradually, giving emphasis here, letting that piece recede and so on. Once again the difficulty is knowing when to stop!

When to use a frame

For certain methods of embroidery it is essential to have the fabric held taut in a frame of some kind. Goldwork and laidwork, for instance, must be worked on a frame to maintain the correct tension. Canvaswork should be framed to prevent distortion and to give ease and rhythm of work (one hand on top and one underneath). Padding and quilting also require framing and special frames are obtainable for these methods at craft shops. For free embroidery, however, use of a frame is more a matter of personal choice. Some stitches, eg chain stitch, would be more difficult if the needle had to be stabbed up and down in a frame.

If you do need to frame your work, it can be pinned out on an old picture frame or on a canvas stretcher, using drawing-pins (thumb tacks) or a staple gun, or you could perhaps use a ring-frame in a particular area. In either case, to avoid marking the work, lay a piece of sheeting over the surface, mount both fabrics together, then cut a hole in the sheeting to expose the embroidery area.

It is advisable to work at a table with the work spread out flat, or the frame resting against it so that both hands are free.

13 DESIGNING A PANEL

So far you have been presented with a dozen different exercises, but this time the choice is yours. Do not let the thirteenth exercise be the unlucky one, the one from which you opt out because the onus is on you! In looking back through the completed exercises, ideas of your own (or at least some embryos) will have emerged. The herringbone, cretan and fly stitches combined with fabrics and other types of stitch might suggest an expression of natural form; perhaps of water, reeds or a pond of waterlilies (see Christine Cooper's panel *Reeds*, page 11), or of winter trees or the growth formation of many types of flowers and shrubs. Couched lines might describe roads on a map, railway lines, a snail shell – what else? French knots and woven wheels could be used in a design of a rockery, the lichen on a crumbling stone wall, etc. How could you extend the use of your satin stitch blocks and seeding stitches – did your stitch samplers help to produce some ideas? How about a bonfire at night? Mark-making, of course, can produce a ready-made design.

In the exercise using fabrics collage along with stitches, we worked from natural form. Look at Joyce Doel's panel *Flowering Cherry* (overleaf):

I have been working on a 'tree' theme for some time: trees on skylines, views through trees, the way changing seasons and the light at different times of day alter the way a tree is perceived.

I sketched this particular blossoming tree, with dark shrubs nearby providing a good tonal contrast, as rain began to fall. There was only time to note the outline and the main areas of contrasting tone, but I felt an immediate urge to record it with fabric and thread.

The cherry tree demanded a strong texture. I tore into narrow strips some fabrics I had loosely tie-dyed (to produce an uneven colour). First attempts to work these strips into French knots were a failure because they would not pass through the various layers of background fabric, but couching the loosely bunched strips into areas of blossom seemed to work well.

You might like to find a piece of driftwood, a cluster of flowers, swans and ducks near the river, etc, and plan a design in which you are working with shapes on a background or one that covers that whole area with colour and stitchery.

We have also taken note of man-made form by working from car wheels; how about a top view of a lemon squeezer? Have a look in the kitchen drawer, or the tool-box, at manhole covers, Victorian architectural features, a crowded shop window. Look also at pictures of places where you have been or things you have seen. One gradually acquires the habit of noticing all sorts of things – it makes life much more interesting!

Making a panel is a new challenge – enjoy it thoroughly and feel satisfaction because it is something all of your own.

The panel *Dove of Peace*, by Heather Gibbs, was the outcome of working through such an introductory course: 'I thought this idea was admirably suitable for a collage and I began playing around with cut pieces of pure silk on a background of slub rayon'. She regrets not having used an embroidery frame when stitching the design on the machine and by hand, but 'One learns by trial and error'.

Teddybears

Dove of Peace by Heather
Gibbs. *26 x 16in (66 x 41cm)*

TO SUM UP...

What have we learned so far? We have handled both threads
and fabrics and considered their textural and tactile qualities.
We have learned how to apply fabrics to a background and to
overlay fine and transparent fabrics. We have also learned to
do a number of different stitches and explored a variety of
ways of using them to give a feeling of stability or movement,
density, texture, etc, and to help integrate fabrics into the
background. We have made use of the sewing-machine as
another enrichment of a design and have learned something
about colours by exploring how they work together.

We may have found it necessary to unpick, discard and alter
what we have done. Unpicking is part of the process; how can
we always be right first time?

We have been selecting and rejecting in making our personal choices, thinking intellectually and feeling intuitively,
and have dealt with a number of technical matters. We have
also done some drawing and designing. We have therefore
established a basis upon which to build and hopefully gained
sufficient enthusiasm and confidence to move on. What we
need now is an extension of possible source material, or starting points for design, and this will be discussed at length in
Chapters 2 and 3.

Flowering Cherry by Joyce
Doel. Inspiration from natural
form. *10¹/₂ x 12in (27 x 30cm)*

CHAPTER 2

FINDING A STARTING POINT

Some time ago I came across a reference to G. Wallas's ideas on creativity. He has suggested there may be four distinct stages in the creative process which he calls preparation, incubation, illumination and verification.

In the first stage of *preparation,* an embroiderer would feel an urge to be looking, touching, thinking about and responding to things they have seen, remembered, etc. It would include making a record by sketching or taking photographs, and also touching and playing with fabrics, threads and other materials.

In the next stage, that Wallas calls *incubation,* it may be far from obvious how best to use an idea that has been recorded and so it might be dropped into the subconscious for a while. I have a number of times made a note or sketch of something unusual and then forgotten about it for months, or even years.

In due course comes *illumination,* that moment of inspiration when you suddenly realise that your sketch would translate beautifully into a piece of canvas work or a patchwork wall-hanging! Now you become much more conscious of the particular qualities both in the subject matter and in the materials themselves. There is usually some special aspect that has impinged. In looking at the sea, one person may be delighted by the qualities of light, another by the pattern and rhythm of the waves. You now begin to translate your notes and sketches into design form and gain a strong idea and feeling of what you want to create.

In the final stage of carrying out the piece of work, many decisions must be made and practical problems resolved – *verification.* Wallas's term is perhaps more applicable to the work of scientists and mathematicians who also experience these stages of creativity, as do writers and musicians, but, in translating our ideas into fabrics and threads, we have to make all the parts work together as a whole and we also feel the need to achieve a kind of truth and completeness.

Quality of subject matter

Bearing these thoughts in mind, it should be emphasised that subject matter and content must be worthy of the effort involved in creating a piece of work: the starting point needs to emerge from our own personal experience and aesthetic feeling in order to have any real significance.

When the source of inspiration is not personal, images can easily become hackneyed. One sees many exhibitions of embroidery and amateur painting in which the renderings of pretty flowers, landscapes, etc, reiterate the expected and accepted ideas of beauty. Such subject matter need not be rejected, but needs to be viewed with a fresh eye and have some special quality to separate it from the clichés of run-of-the-mill work.

Avoid inventing a vaguely remembered form; search for something that is meaningful to you. If you wish to embroider a tree, why not step outside and look at one!

We are inundated with images on television and in magazines; endless advertisements of glamorised people, cars, cruise ships, fancy food and exotic landscapes. It is difficult to resist their smooth sophistication and keep faith in our own ability to say something personal and worthwhile, but we should try.

The following two pieces both have a strong sense of individuality and of having something to 'say'.

The first piece is by Rozanne Pibworth Hawksley

Glass-lidded box, covered and lined with red silk taffeta and trimmed with silver/gilt lace. The glove hand is of fine white kid, the back stitched with gold thread, pearls and sequins. The cuff is of white silk satin and lined with pink taffeta and trimmed with

Playground

Autumn Leaves: lithograph

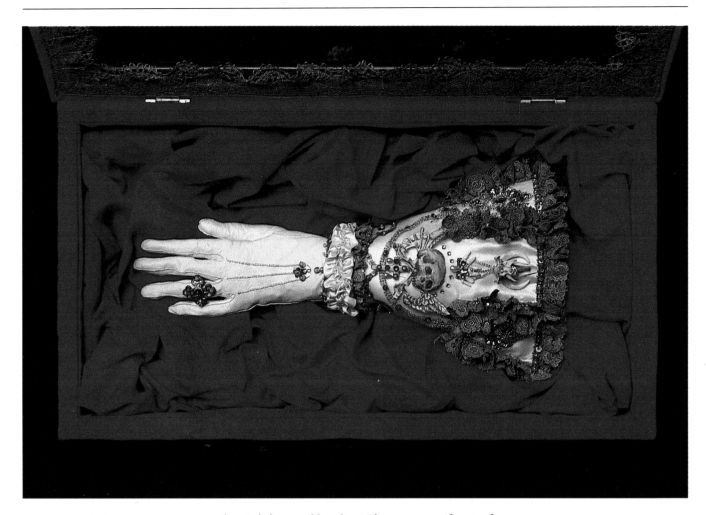

... et ne nos inducas ...
(... and lead us not ...) by
Rozanne Pibworth Hawksley.
13 x 23 x 5¹/₂in
(33 x 58 x 14cm)

silver/gilt lace and beading. The main motifs are of bone, painted or set with jewels and represent the Holy Spirit descending, offering man the Crown of Life and Free Will; the choice between good and evil; the triumph of good through Christ's death (his five wounds and tears).

In contrast, Clem Gilder's work displays a wry humour

The inspiration for this panel derived from my involvement in catering and my experiences during those years, in particular my observations of people in relation to others and to their surroundings.

I had several ideas for various scenes but finally chose the restaurant with the over-indulgent customer and ever-patronising head waiter!

The panel was worked almost entirely in felt. This was dyed and the details then added using an airbrush. The background was worked in one piece, with the figures and architectural details applied on to it. The faces and hands of the figures were worked using tights (panty hose); the features were created by hand stitching, then coloured using an airbrush. The bodies were pieced together and finally each complete character was slip-stitched on to the scene.

The following section is intended to help you think about and look for starting points in embroidery. As creative results depend on an open and enquiring attitude, it is often helpful to focus for a time on some particular area of experience and to search for different aspects which are of special interest to you.

We begin by looking at our surroundings in both the natural and man-made world, learning to select those aspects

that interest us particularly. In recording our impressions in sketches, notes or photographs, certain visual aspects will seem important, perhaps the quality of light, feeling of rhythm, or mood of the occasion. We may be very factual and analytical, or free and expressive, according to the subject matter and how we feel about it.

Alternatively we may be inspired by work seen in art galleries or museums and again will need to make notes about things that appeal to us.

Ways of designing other than from observation are suggested, which include playing with letters cut directly from folded paper or fabric, mark-making, manipulating fabrics and threads in different ways and working from geometric form.

Idea-based work is also considered, in which particular topics or themes provide starting points for individual or group work in embroidery.

Anything Else Sir? by Clem Gilder. *44in (112cm) square*

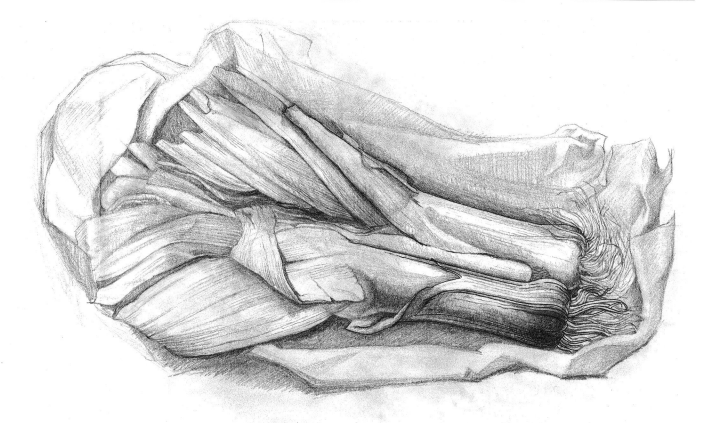

Original drawing for **Calico Leek,** with the finished piece

PRIMARY SOURCES

To use a primary source means working directly from the actual object, scene, etc. It could be done by sitting there and stitching straight into the fabric, just as a painter will set up an easel and start painting. It can also take the form of making a record by such means as seems most appropriate and then designing from the resulting sketch or photograph.

It is surprising how often sensitive, worthwhile and able work is produced from scrappy and minimal sketches. Putting down an idea on paper is a great stumbling block for many people and yet, when faced with fabrics and threads, they will work with great confidence and careful thinking.

An impressive sketch is not essential, and your initial notes are private unless you choose to show them. The rough notes you make in response to your looking are likely to capture the special quality that caught your attention, and, if you concentrate on trying to put down essential features plus written notes, you may very well find that this is sufficient.

Some people, of course, draw quite happily and this is a great advantage as in learning to draw they have learned to see. It is the seeing that is so important.

Natural form

This is a much favoured source of inspiration. How can we step beyond the habitual images that spring to mind in landscapes, flower drawings, etc?

Perhaps it is a good idea to go somewhere new. This gives a

sense of adventure and increases our interest and curiosity.

Kate Davis says of her panel *Woodland Heritage* (overleaf):

This work developed from sketches of an ancient sawn-off tree trunk in the depths of the country. I tried to evoke a woodland atmosphere and to give the feeling of regeneration in such a setting.

The piece is a combination of smocking and canvas work; the fabrics and threads have been dyed to blend the colours subtly.

Ceramic pieces have been included to make an interesting contrast in texture and to develop the theme of natural materials wood, earth, clay, silk, etc.

The canvas work stitches have been used sparingly and the smocked fabric shaped to exaggerate the fluid lines and textures seen in the source material. Hand-painted and rolled paper beads decorate the tassels.

It is interesting to explore contrasts of scale: the great archway of rock which dwarfs a person to an insignificant dot, huge leaves like giant rhubarb as large as armchairs, or the flowing leafy pattern of a Virginia creeper. Examine them carefully, note how the leaves join the stem and the way the tendrils search for a strong grip to haul themselves up the wall.

Notice the outline shapes of trees. These characteristics of shape and growth make them identifiable from a distance. Many trees appear as a dense shape in summer while others, such as cedar, ash and silver birch, are more open, with the sky visible through the branches and the leaves in separate clusters. These variations of shape, colour and rhythm add great richness to the scene.

Think what aspects of nature make a particular appeal to you. Look at the view, or at a piece of moss; water, fire, earth, sky, clouds, plants, people, animals, birds, fish, reptiles, insects, shells, etc. Remember that the changing seasons offer differences in light and atmosphere. Remember also that 'my cat' is usually more significant than 'a cat'.

The recording of natural form could involve drawing or painting in a medium of your choice. (See Chapter 6 for information about drawing materials and suggestions on how to start work.) This could be on a large scale or very small. You might spend an afternoon making a careful study, or ten minutes jotting down the most significant features. You might prefer to take photographs from different positions or some close-ups. Whichever way you make your record, you will need to translate your ideas into your medium at a later stage.

Man-made form

In this changing world people who are not necessarily involved in the technological aspects of life may nevertheless find relationships of form and pattern in the man-made world both interesting, inspiring and a new extension of their visual awareness. So where shall we look for these new ideas?

Ours is an era of fast travel. Motorways have road signs, fly overs, spaghetti junctions, and service areas for petrol and food, with parking for cars and the huge lorries of today. Boats and ships can offer glimpses of machinery, ropes, folded sails, funnels. Often a small section as seen through one's cupped hands can offer an interesting focus.

There is an endless provision of subject material that we can easily overlook, eg the display of goods at the chemist shop, a heap of boxes in the supermarket or a pile of toys in the children's bedroom.

Rock archway dwarfing the human figure

Outline shape of an elm tree

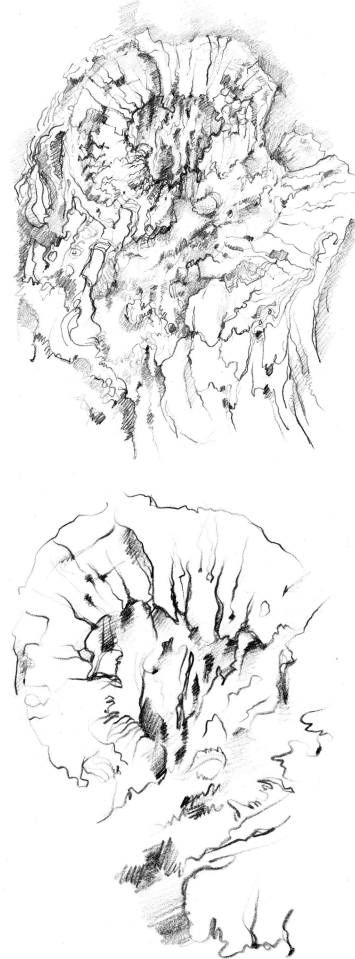

Drawings for **Woodland Heritage** by Kate Davis

Woodland Heritage by Kate Davis, using smocking, canvas work and some ceramic pieces. *15 x 16¹/₂in (38 x 42cm)*

Ephelandra on a Chair by
Elsie Faulkner

We can look at scaffolding and buildings wrapped in polythene sheeting, amazingly ornate Victorian facades or artisan cottages, contrasts of decaying walls overgrown with healthy weeds, the debris on a building site, dustbins, cranes, chairs stacked in lecture halls, the church organ, or the local bar. It is not necessary to use the whole thing, parts and details make good potential design material.

Cities today have many high-rise blocks with their myriad of windows, some totally blank, others illuminated with strip lights. We see buildings with reflective glass, returning surprising pictures of clouds where one was expecting steel and concrete! Blocks of flats have balconies, interesting fire escapes, unusual wall openings. Some city banks and large stores have a great atrium and criss-crossing escalators with infinite reflections in mirrors.

This is creative looking, noticing shape against shape, the colours, the effect of light and the textures to be seen everywhere about us. With this freshness of vision you will not be producing yet another patchwork of the New York skyline!

The modes of recording will be similar to those used in response to natural form.

Isabel del Strother's panel *Look at Florence* (overleaf) was enlarged from a 4½in (11.5cm) square photograph taken from a window in the Vasari Corridor looking over the Ponte Vecchio into the town centre. She has used a calico background and some dye; single strands in various shades of stranded cotton produce the rich textures of the buildings and couched threads are used on the roofs. The frame is covered in stone-coloured stretch-towelling.

SECONDARY SOURCES

Using secondary sources as a starting point for one's own work means deriving inspiration from an image or an object made by someone else. With this in mind we can look at the work of artists, craftsmen and designers from the past and present, to be found in art galleries, museums or elsewhere. Modern life also presents us with a flood of photographic images which may offer worthwhile source material.

It is necessary to judge the quality of source material, to select the first-rate from the banal. Perhaps, though, it is the banal quality that has captured your attention! Roy Lichtenstein's art is based on comic strips, Andy Warhol has painted a can of Coca-Cola. The important aspect here is the awareness and intention; to choose the banal without realising is quite another matter. Even worthy material can be copied or translated in a way that is superficial and trivialising; one's judgement improves with experience and increasing sensitivity.

When researching a subject using secondary sources go to the original if possible and, if not, use good photographs or analytical drawings from a book.

Inspiration from galleries and museums
What are the ways in which the art and craft of past or present can be a source of inspiration to the embroiderer?

On the one hand it provides us with secondary source material. It can also give us the opportunity to develop personal understanding of values in art and craft in terms of the kind of knowledge, skills and aesthetic judgement involved in its making. Awareness of the way in which art and craftworks

Criss-crossing escalators

Interior by Gordon Faulkner

47

Look at Florence by Isabel del
Strother, an inspiration from
the man-made world. *17in
(43cm) square*

Seaside, a patchwork wall-
hanging, inspired by a print by
Edwardo Paolozzi. *46 x 65in
(117 x 160cm)*

are created, how styles evolve and change. can help embroiderers (working at whatever level) achieve a stronger sense of their place in history and also offer direction and motivation.

Let us consider the use of art or craft as secondary source material. While looking at works of past or present for whatever reason, in an open, receptive way, we may suddenly feel the urge to explore a particular possibility in our own work. Sometimes this feeling comes later, as we reflect on the experience. The important thing now is to make sure we use the idea or element from the artist's work in a creative, personal way.

As usual, a record will need to be made. At a later date, after these ideas have come to fruition, we may wish to return and learn more about the work in terms of its history and social context but, at the time, it is the striking quality of the image that is significant.

To give an instance of this, some years ago a print by the Scottish artist Paolozzi made me think of patchwork. After making a few notes and sketches of some units he had used, and after a process of playing with and developing some of these, I designed and made the patchwork wall-hanging *Seaside,* which was quite my own. Several strip patchwork ideas were explored on squared paper until this one was eventually selected. It was then enlarged to size on cartridge paper. Strip patchwork has been combined with other shapes in most sections of the design, which was pieced by machine or by hand, as seemed most appropriate at each stage. Borders of log-cabin type strips frame the work.

Let us now look at ways in which art can be used as secondary source material for our own work.

There seem to be three ways in which this can be done. Firstly, some people imitate subject matter, styles, conventions and techniques of original works so exactly that it is difficult to distinguish them from the original work. What is

the point of this, apart from running a remunerative business in fakes?

A second way is to study the work of a particular artist, make use of certain features and adapt them to one's own choice of subject matter, methods and materials, and evolve one's own style and conventions. I have worked in this way by responding to the paintings of Matisse: using his type of colours, decorative qualities and rhythms, applying them to a life-drawing made in pastels and then translating this drawing into the large patchwork wall-hanging *Boy, Seated* (p53).

I first made a careful tracing of the drawing and had it enlarged on a photocopying machine to double its size. It was particularly important that the black outlines should be enlarged correctly. The colours were matched accurately in cotton fabrics which were pieced to match the design and applied on to a black cotton backing. This was then cut away in order that the paper templates could be extracted. Eventually this 'top' was laid over a layer of padding and a backing fabric and quilted on either side of the black lines, and elsewhere as appropriate, on the sewing-machine, then finished off with the log-cabin borders.

A third way of using art objects is to extract particular units or motifs from a piece of work and integrate them in a new, honest and personal manner. This is the way the Paolozzi print was used as inspiration for *Seaside.*

Traditional crafts

In looking at craftwork, we are very soon aware that from the earliest times there has been an impulse to make and create objects in which the thought and the care taken go far beyond the basic utilitarian aspects. Some have symbolic meaning and others embody a desire to make something with a unity of form and decoration that is right for the job to be done. Some are richly embellished, others are economical in their statement. This urge seems universal and it still persists today.

It is interesting to look at crafts other than one's own, as Diana Parkes of New Zealand has done in her piece *Chameleon* (overleaf):

> Research into shield shapes and their usage led me to their indirect application as body adornment.

Moore of Me card by Sarah Hosking

Camel and Bull from *Animal Regalia* by Moira Broadbent

Although basically decorative, the shapes and patterns that evolved became challenging and expressive. While not actually structured to be worn, they are envisaged as representing an embellishment or outer covering over other garments. They are suggestive of status symbols, where class distinction and the hierarchical system presents itself with the outward sign of clothing and adornment. In doing so the wearer and the viewer are segregated, each to their own systems – the body adornment acting as a shield and a claim to that division. The inspiration and design for each piece of work usually commences with a vague idea and the work progresses intuitively. Fabrics used, apart from the blacks, are hand-dyed using a number of dye techniques. The background is dyed embroidery canvas 13 threads to the inch. All hang softly from painted wood rods.

Valerie Tulloch writes of her panel *Inspiration for Embroidery*:

A series of hand embroideries using simple straight and chain stitches on calico resulted from my suddenly seeing with fresh eyes a familiar knitted patchwork blanket draped over a chair. Contrasts of colour against black and white had always appealed to me so in the first small interpretation the chair and surroundings were in fine black lines with the solid chain-stitched blanket in colour. Different options were tried, then followed studies of a different chair, blanket and setting, all with strong personal associations. This straightforward representation with quilted outlines and chain stitches worked solidly in varying directions pays tribute to my mother, the knitter, to writers of books and to unknown embroiderers and textile artists.

We might decide to use motifs from architecture, basketry or other crafts we have studied as source material for our own work. We should try to respect their character by using them creatively in ways suited to the methods, materials and purposes of today. In dress embroidery, for instance, by the choices we make in the colour and texture of fabrics and threads, beads, etc, and the scale and positioning of the motifs used, we should hope to achieve an essential 'rightness' equivalent to the qualities we enjoyed in the craftwork we studied.

Other crafts, such as pottery, jewellery, wood-engraving, illumination of manuscripts, weaving, etc, are also worth studying for pleasure and for inspiration; you will have your own preferences.

Looking at past and present embroidery

Embroidery has a long and impressive history, embracing at different times and in various places the making of both simple craft objects and of fine artworks. It has been used in the decoration of palaces and great houses and as a display of wealth and status in the clothing of royalty and nobility in many parts of the world. It has also been made and used in the humblest cottages where, for instance, patchwork and quilting have offered a means of using scraps and hardworn fabrics to create warm bedcovers. People, mostly women, have made table-mats, cushion covers, babies' bonnets and gowns, ecclesiastical robes and banners, displaying the love of making and creating beautiful things to be seen and used. We will give infinite time and care for the pleasure of doing and the enrichment of the environment.

Here then, is an immense variety of source material for study and inspiration.

Some people are fascinated by stitchery, both how to do particular stitches and the study of ways in which they have been used. Pursuing this interest could cross boundaries of periods and regions. Other people might be interested in the embroidery of a particular country and that could span the categories of costume, book covers, bed hangings, whitework and so on, covering a great variety of methods and materials. Again, some will make a study of objects of some kind such as gloves, or pincushions, while others will study a method such as cut-work, whitework, or the making of cords and tassels.

The aims involved can vary considerably. One person might pursue a historical search for the pleasure of discovering and examining the pieces and yet never wish to handle a needle.

Others enjoy collecting work of different types and an initial interest can become a very serious pursuit. Moira Broadbent's collection of animal regalia led her to research the history and religions of different peoples, to make a study of the way they lived and the animals for which they created their rich embroideries and weaving. All this provided the

Chameleon by Diana Parkes of New Zealand. One of a series of panels following her research into shapes.
14 x 16in (35 x 41cm)

basis for a book on the subject to accompany the travelling exhibition of her collection (see Bibliography).

Many people look at embroidery collections, both historical and recent, in order to extend their ideas on the possibilities within a favourite method (such as goldwork or stumpwork) and study design, technique, materials and stitches and how they have been used, then experiment with what they have learnt in subsequent pieces of work.

Studying various traditional methods such as cutwork, reverse appliqué, Florentine embroidery, needleweaving, etc, may lead to work in these methods appropriate to today, perhaps varying the scale, the materials and type of threads used, etc.

Great interest is developing in the study of textiles from Africa, India and the East, etc, of which many have a great richness and brilliance of colour. A student may study a sample of work such as a piece of Indian embroidery enriched with Shisha glass and either make a series of drawings or a close copy in fabrics, thus becoming much more aware of the technical processes and aesthetic qualities of the work. These studies will then offer inspiration for quite new and exciting work of their own.

As well as studying historical or ethnic embroidery, it is interesting and important to visit exhibitions of present-day work, which has been inspired by all manner of different sources, and also to look at work in allied textile crafts such as felt-making, weaving, fashion in dress, etc. The originality and

Boy seated A patchwork wall-
hanging in response to colours
and rhythms in the work of
Matisse. *42 x 55in (1.07 x 1.40m)*

the new approaches show that the textile arts and crafts are in a very healthy state.

Jean Draper's panel *Overlapping Triangles* (overleaf) is one of a series of works resulting from a visit to India. Peeling and faded patterns on palace walls and overlapping images caused by looking through decorative screens, archways and windows have been the main source of inspiration. The background is slubbed silk in a typically hot Indian pink, to which the basic square was added in gold leaf. On to this were applied rows of triangles made from machine embroidery in silk and metal thread on soluble fabric with hand embroidery and beads added. Bronze powders were used in places to soften the brightness of the gold leaf. Overlapping triangles made from organza with an application of gold fabric paint, and an edge of running stitch in fine gold threads, were suspended above the surface surrounding the bright centre.

To cut out a letter 'O'

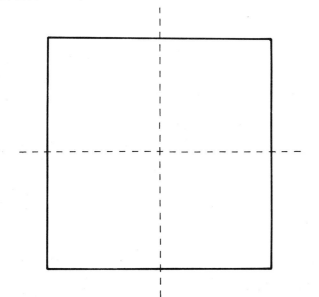

Take a square of paper and fold it into four

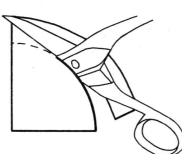

Decide on the thickness of the 'O' and cut a second arc, parallel with the first

LETTERING

Lettering offers an excellent source of design, not just for making words, but also for the beauty of the simple shapes. To cut out an alphabet by the direct means offered here (many thanks to Donald Quantrill, calligrapher, for teaching it to me) and then to push the paper letters around is an excellent way to practise positioning them or, alternatively, to forget about their significance and have fun by producing patterns with mass-produced cut-letter shapes that vary in their sizes and in the thickness of stroke.

Designing lettering is a highly skilled area of expertise and amateur efforts at trying to draw and paint letters can look very clumsy and insensitive, yet when simple letter forms are cut directly from folded paper or fabric without previous drawing, they can achieve a particular vitality. Because cut shapes can be moved about, the crucial problem of spacing can be overcome without endless drawing and rubbing out.

The block letters in this section are based on the traditional proportions of the Roman alphabet, but without the subtle refinements. The diagrams, of course, have to be drawn accurately, which may seem a contradiction of the spontaneous approach but great liveliness and individuality does result from this very quick way of working.

The principle used is explained in the diagrams for cutting the letter 'O'.

This principle applies to all the letters. In the following diagrams the whole letter is drawn, but the heavy line and dark grey tone show the first folding and cutting. In some cases there is a second operation to perform, as in the letter C: having cut an 'O' as before, you now partially unfold it, as shown by the light grey area, and cut away more paper to translate an 'O' into a 'C.'

In some of the diagrams, eg M, W, S and N, some of the construction lines used to obtain a correct thickness for the stroke have been left, so if at some time you wish to draw the letters carefully, you will understand how to do so.

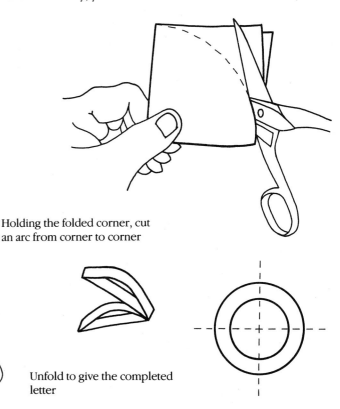

Holding the folded corner, cut an arc from corner to corner

Unfold to give the completed letter

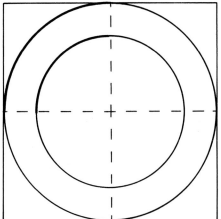

Cutting 'whole' letters. Start with a square of paper

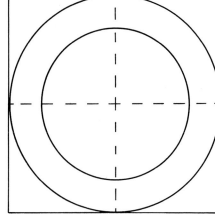

To make a 'C', first cut an 'O', open in half. Then cut as shown

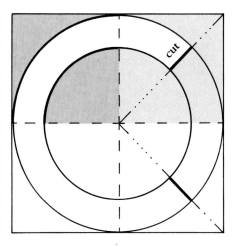

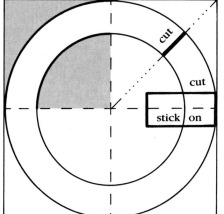

To make a 'G', first cut an 'O', open out fully, then cut as shown. Stick on strip as shown

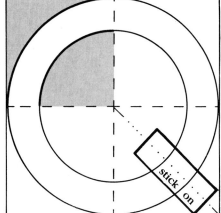

To make a 'Q', first cut an 'O', then stick on strip as shown

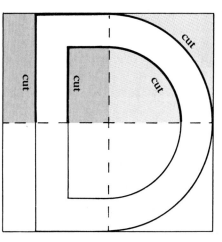

To make a 'D', quarter fold the paper, then open to half; fold and cut as shown

To make an 'M', fold in half and cut as shown (dotted lines show construction lines)

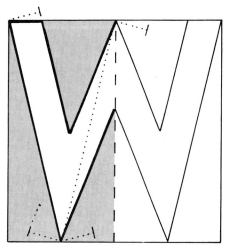

To make a 'W', fold in half and cut as shown (dotted lines show construction lines)

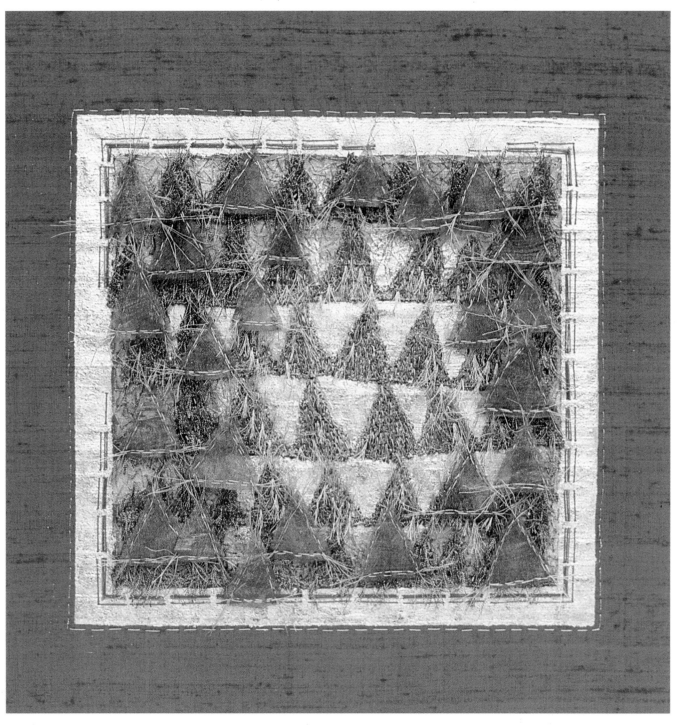

Overlapping Triangles by Jean Draper. This piece was in response to a visit to India. *14in (36cm) square*

(opposite)
Inspiration for Embroidery by Valerie Tulloch, resulting from her suddenly seeing a familiar knitted patchwork blanket with fresh eyes. *14 x 18¹⁄₂in (36 x 47cm)*

A basic alphabet
The alphabet is divided into three basic types of letter as follows.
'Whole' letters, based on a square:
O C G Q D M W
'Three-quarter' letters, the width being ³⁄₄ of the height:
H U V A N T Z X
(These are easy to remember as they make a sort of word.)
'Half' letters, the width being ¹⁄₂ of the height:
B E F I J K L P R S Y
Use gummed coloured paper or newspaper at this experimental stage. Cut directly and do not worry about any slight points on your circle. Slight variations are part of the character of the method, but try to keep the 'thickness' of the strokes as even as possible. In the diagrams the thickness is ¹⁄₆th of the height, but you could choose your own proportions.

An example of a 'whole' letter O 'three-quarter' letter A and 'half' letter K

Cutting 'three-quarter' letters. Start with a rectangle three-quarters the width of the original square, but the same height

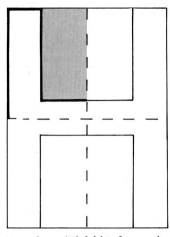

To make an 'H', fold in four and cut as shown

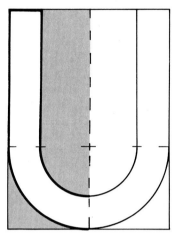

To make a 'U', fold in half vertically and cut as shown

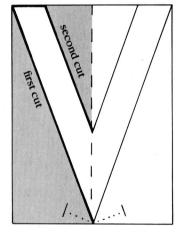

To make a 'V', fold in half vertically and cut as shown

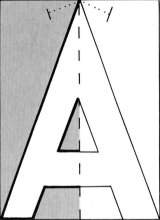

To make an 'A', fold in half vertically and cut as shown

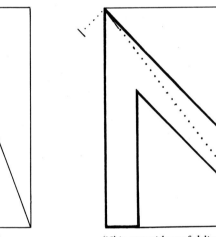

'N' is cut without folding

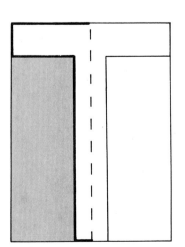

To make a 'T', fold in half vertically and cut as shown

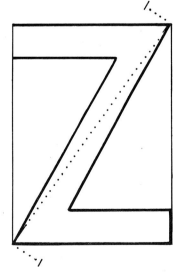

'Z' is cut without folding

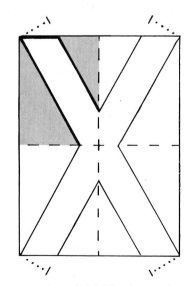

To make an 'X', fold in four and cut as shown

Cutting 'half' letters. Start with a rectangle half the width of the original square, but the same height

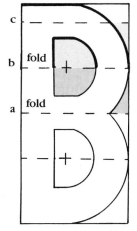 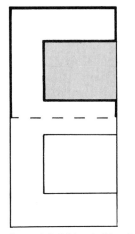 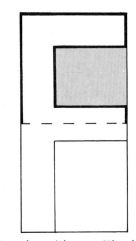 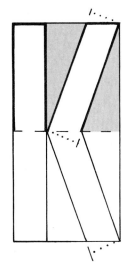

To make a 'B', fold in half at (a), then fold at (b) to take (a) up to (c). Cut as shown, following on above (c)

To make an 'E', fold in half and cut as shown

To make an 'F', cut an 'E' and remove foot

To make a 'K', fold in half and cut as shown

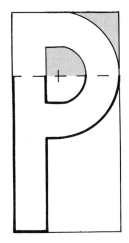 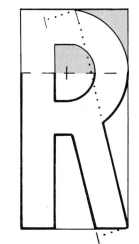 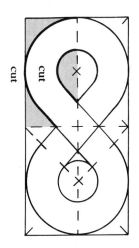 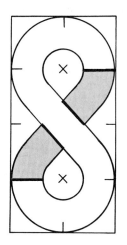

To make a 'P', fold top quarter down and cut as shown

To make an 'R', fold top quarter down, cut centre as shown, then cut remainder as shown

'S' is cut in two stages. Fold in four and cut as shown. Open

out fully and cut out remaining areas

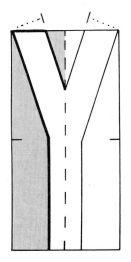 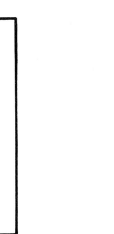 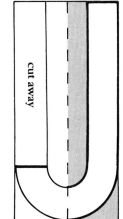 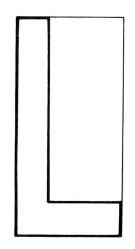

To make a 'Y', fold in half vertically and cut as shown

To make an 'I', cut as shown

To make a 'J', fold in half vertically, cut, then open out and cut away as shown

To make an 'L', cut as shown

WORKING DIRECTLY FROM MATERIALS

Working directly from materials means working without any preliminary sketches or preconceived ideas of an end result. It is a 'hands-on' approach which challenges our inventiveness, our desire to explore and to do something different.

This can take a number of different forms, ranging from mark-making and finger painting, which are mainly two-dimensional approaches, to the handling of any kind of materials, two or three-dimensional, with a view to exploring their potential as expressive art media.

MARK-MAKING

Some of you will already have tried your hand at some simple mark-making in Chapter 1. Here are some further suggestions of ways of working in this area.

Finger painting by a student following a general art course, an example of mark-making

Cats: thumb prints by Sarah Hosking

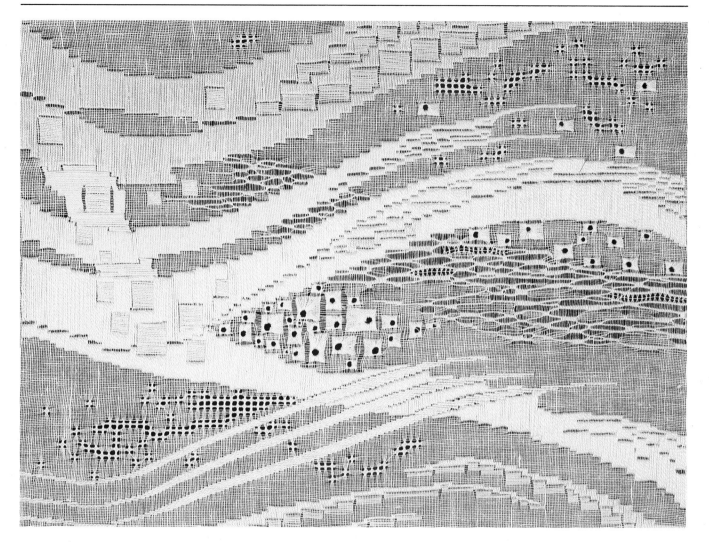

It can be interesting to find a source of inspiration by some means other than working from observation. For people who feel shy of trying their hand at drawing, working from different types of 'mark-making' can be a direct way of starting to design and one likely to diminish inhibitions. This literally means making marks on paper by various means. For those happy to draw and paint, it can offer an alternative approach which opens up fresh possibilities and may suggest new ways of using line and texture.

Using black paint only is often the most successful way to work, but try colour if you wish, though pale colours like yellow tend to give disappointing results. It is worthwhile covering many large sheets of paper such as cheap newsprint with substantial areas of each type of mark. Several ways of mark-making follow, and then you can invent your own.

White Rhythms Mark-making translated into pulled threadwork and satin stitch. *21 x 15¹/₂in (53 x 39cm)*

Mark-making: starting point for *White Rhythms*

Stampings and printings etc
Using thick poster paint and a big brush, paint the end of a match-box and press it on paper. Dilute the paint to a suitable consistency, then make a great many marks: densely, then thinning out, lying in different directions, overlapping, printed in neat rows, or used to create a feeling of movement.

Try using the ends of felt-tipped pens, cotton reels, cardboard tubes etc, twigs or other found objects. Stencil through a mesh, eg embroidery or rug canvas. Drop some rather wet paint on paper, fold it over and press it and perhaps add further blots later. Try splashing paint on damp paper and letting it run in different directions, or blowing paint through a straw. Combine several of these approaches,

Mark-making: combed paint

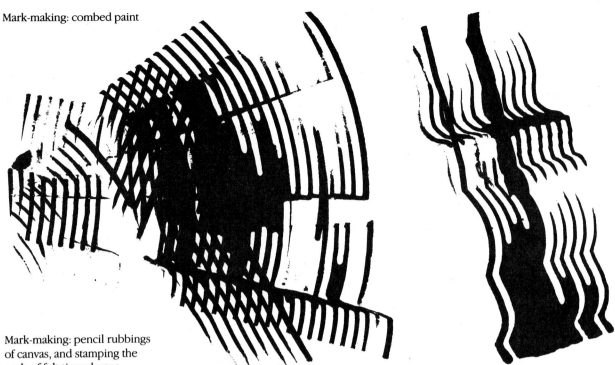

Mark-making: pencil rubbings
of canvas, and stamping the
ends of felt-tipped pens

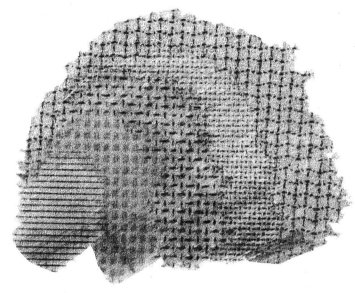

or tear out several different pieces and collage them together, perhaps on black or grey paper. To avoid producing clichés, it is important that you also search for your own choice of objects for this exercise.

Rubbings
Using fairly thin, but strong paper, and charcoal, conté crayons or greasy crayons, lay the paper over some textured surface such as the reverse side of hardboard, tree bark, bricks, wood grain, etc, and rub quite hard and very closely to produce areas of texture. If there is too great a depth to the surface you are working on the paper will tear, but you will soon discover what will work and what will not. (See the collage of rubbing, *Jugs and Teapots,* on page 184.)

Combed paint
Paint the teeth of a comb and draw great flowing curves or overlapping lines, etc. Keep exploring and do large enough areas of each type of mark so that the rhythm and pattern will begin to emerge. Cover several large sheets in this way.

Finger painting
If you feel inhibited about painting, it is interesting and fun to try painting freely with your fingers, using poster colour mixed with wall-papering paste on large sheets of cheap cartridge paper size A2 or, better still, A1. Mix up quite a lot of the paste in several jam jars and add a different colour of poster paint to each.

Start by pouring about a tablespoonful of just one colour on the paper and pushing it about with your finger tips. Try standing up to work and move your arms from the elbows, then from the shoulders, so you make great swirling lines and rhythms. Keep on for a long time, overlapping your lines and changing directions. Now add other colours and see what happens. Try exploring the possibilities of contrasting strengths of colour, of mixing colours and the creation of texture.

The aim is not to produce a picture of a scene or an object, it is to appreciate the quality of lines and marks for their own sake. It is quite therapeutic and may also produce some interesting design possibilities!

Developing your mark-making

Examine your sheets of mark-making for areas that are especially interesting, perhaps because they suggest a feeling of rhythm and movement, or because they offer a rich textural quality inviting translation into embroidery.

Using a small 'window' cut out of a postcard, work over your different sheets, isolating any areas that look promising and framing them with a pencilled square, rectangle or circle, as seems appropriate. These could be translated into stitchery samples, or perhaps offer the start of a full-scale design.

I have created spontaneous designs with marks of different kinds which, when enlarged, translated directly into collages of transparent fabrics, machine embroidery and hand stitchery, the depth and richness of which were indicated by the qualities of the mark-making. In one instance – *White Rhythms* – a tiny area about 5cm across turned into a panel ten times its size, in pulled threadwork on white scrim. This was an attempt to make a flowing design within the discipline of this counted method, using cotton threads in four thicknesses which varied in their whiteness and sheen. Moyra McNeill's book *Pulled Thread* (see Bibliography) was an excellent source, especially for her exciting use of satin stitch of varying tensions. This was the main stitch used, along with free eyelets and mock faggot filling. To achieve a smooth flowing line a block had to be stepped up in the broad areas of satin stitch, either on the top or on the bottom line, but never both at once. Some areas of horizontal stitchery gave variety by reflecting the light differently. I felt that the piece managed to extend the boundaries of this traditional method.

Even if you do not pursue your mark-making beyond the paint stage, it may well increase your visual awareness, so you will observe and enjoy the many marks and textures of our everyday world.

Collage print

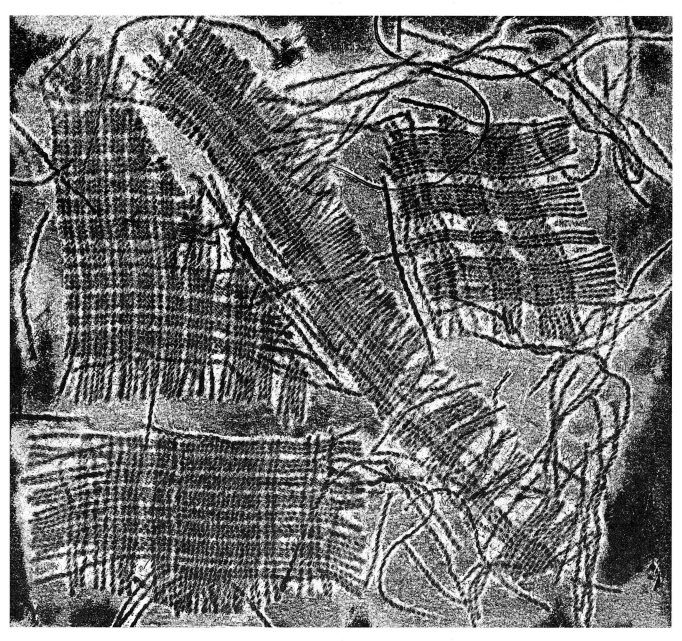

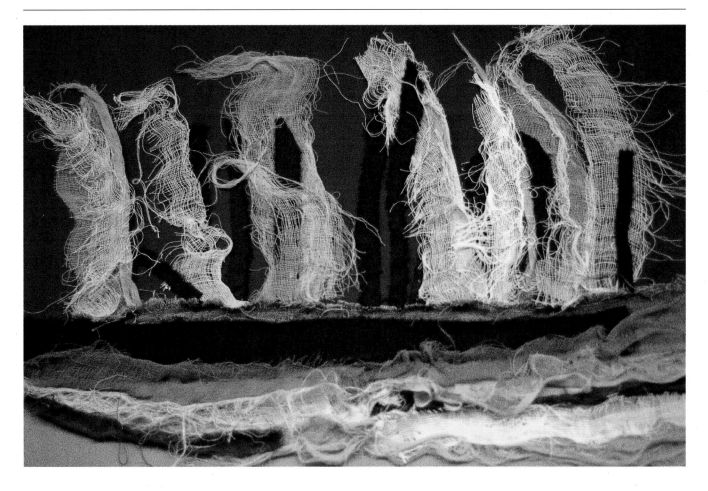

MANIPULATION OF FABRICS, THREADS AND OTHER MATERIALS

Working directly from materials in the field of embroidery begins with the collection of miscellaneous fabrics, threads and less obvious materials such as off-cuts of wood, chicken wire, cardboard, dowelling rods, plastic bags, string, polystyrene, plastic fencing or anything else you can find. Select a few things from the pile and sit quietly touching them, grouping them and allowing them to suggest possibilities to you; then try out your ideas.

This may seem to stretch the concept of embroidery to an extreme; ultimately it is up to the individual to decide how far they wish to go, but an open-minded approach produces vitality and, as you will see, these ideas can be found in the work of textile artists today. Increasingly the boundaries are breaking down between areas such as embroidery, weaving, paper-making, painting and printing and, as these crafts overlap, new terms such as 'fibre art' come into use and new and exciting possibilities emerge.

Initially we will explore some of these ideas by producing a number of varied samplers. It is important that these pieces be collected and mounted, as a record for future reference and as visual aids for teaching. It is all too easy to push oddments of work to the back of a drawer and forget them!

Extracting threads from fabrics

A favourite exercise of the sixties and seventies was to take a loosely woven fabric such as hessian, draw out threads from warp, weft or both, and to use various drawn threadwork stitches and techniques (but on a scale much larger than on the fine linen tablecloths made by our grandmothers). Threads used might be those extracted from the fabric, or quite different ones of varied colour, thickness and texture. Alternatively bundles of threads, strips of felt, etc, were woven back into the spaces. Twigs, grasses, string and metal strips were also used with beech nuts, rose hips, nuts and bolts, wooden beads etc, added as decoration.

Another exercise was to make a vertical cut several inches long in a piece of hessian and to draw back the horizontal threads, leaving a framed square or rectangle of the warp threads, with loose threads at either side that could be darned back, or made into plaits or tassels. The central area offered an opportunity for needleweaving, using self-coloured threads or others, and producing patterns or images such as trees, often with a coloured background laid behind.

Eventually so many people had done these exercises that they took on a 'period' look; one felt that every possible idea had been explored. Yet these exercises were valid and can still offer a voyage of discovery. Why not rethink these now traditional methods in terms of today, by working with different types of fabric?

Woollen tweeds sometimes have one colour in the warp and another in the weft. We could draw out a number of weft threads, replacing them with a bundle of threads from the warp and vice versa, weaving them through, say, every sixth thread. This alone would change the character of the fabric. We could stitch narrow strips of the same fabric across the surface and fray the edges; if the strips were cut in the opposite direction, the frayed edges would be in the other colour! Another idea might be to insert painted wooden rods where threads had been removed.

Forest Fire by Anne Boutle. An experiment with torn and tucked cotton scrim.
23¹/₂ x 14¹/₂in (60 x 37cm)

The surfaces could then be enriched with the use of stitchery, beads, ribbons and cords, and the application of contrasting fabrics.

Extracting threads from fine fabrics such as muslin would give a delicate look and it could be interesting, though time-consuming, to draw out threads from very fine fabrics like silk.

Another possibility is to fray edges, or to remove nearly all the threads leaving a small, possibly irregular, central area. If the fabric has a printed design, the centre could be padded following the lines of the design, the loose threads laid out on a background and couched down in rhythms which relate to the central feature and the whole enriched with stitchery.

Some fabrics like cotton scrim and tarlatan can be fringed and pulled into new shapes and mounted on background fabrics.

Look at all sorts of fabrics, and see what ideas they can suggest to you.

The fabric collage *Forest Fire* (opposite), by Anne Boutle, was inspired by a colour plate in an old book called *Paddle to the Sea*. The background fabric is maroon twill and beige polyester, cut lengths of dark green crimplene represent the trees and river and torn scrim is used for the flames. In the lower half of the panel the scrim is torn and tucked for the reflections of flames in the water. All the fabrics are attached with small tacking stitches.

See also the detail of Dorothy Wood's panel *Winter Solstice*:

My inspiration was the centre of a pear-shape worked on a calico sampler. I wanted to try out the drawn threadwork on a larger scale and, after tacking round a 12in (30cm) circle on stretched muslin, I cut the weft threads very carefully and using a fine strong needle pulled out all the threads on the right hand side. These were woven back into the muslin for ¹/₂in (1cm). The work began to resemble a winter sun or moon. I began to experiment by pulling the other threads gently with a tapestry needle until I was satisfied with the effect. A torn-paper template was used to screen-print a 'sun behind clouds', then both pieces of muslin were stapled on to a white painted frame, 23¹/₂in (60cm) square. The rough edges were finished with a band of muslin and hemmed in place. The embroidery was finished with needleweaving on the warp threads and the loose threads were held in place with fabric stiffener.

Pulled threads

Another possibility in playing with fabrics is to move threads in loosely-woven materials, either by stitching them tightly in places or pushing them close together in groups (the method used for the panel *White Rhythms*).

Carole Waddle has explored pulled thread techniques with machine embroidery in a totally different way in her project *Glasshouses and Greenhouses* (overleaf), based on photographs and drawings of leaves and stems reflected in water at Kew gardens.

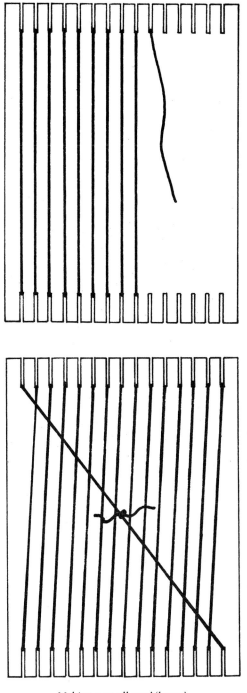

Making a small card 'loom', showing string knotted at the back

Experimental weaving

If you have explored the construction of fabrics as suggested in the last exercise, you may now be interested in weaving some of your own.

Let us begin by making some small card 'looms' about A4 in size; the card used must be strong. Make slits along the top

(left)
Winter Solstice by Dorothy
Wood. An example of both
extracting threads and 'pulling'
them using fine muslin. *23¹/₂in
(60cm) square x 1¹/₂in (3cm)
deep*

and bottom edges, 1cm apart and 1cm in depth, but leaving a
2cm margin at either side, ie fifteen slots.

Cards of A1 size can be cut into eight pieces, piled into a
block and the slots cut with a saw, thereby producing enough
for a class quite quickly.

Using string that is fairly fine and very strong, thread the
warp from top to bottom and up over the back into the next
slot. Leave long ends and, after you have checked that the tension is fairly tight and quite even, tie the two ends together
firmly with a knot, on the back of the card.

Now, using a big tapestry needle, or a long weaving needle,
and beginning at the bottom, weave a plain smooth thread of
suitable colour over and under the warp threads. At the end
of the row change direction and work over the threads you
went under in the last row. At the end of each row, stretch the
work sideways to allow the weft thread to lie fairly loosely, so
ensuring an even tension. Work several rows like this and do
the same at the top as you finish off, to produce firm edges.
The weft threads can be pushed more closely together using a
fork or a comb.

When you have finished your sampler, darn the loose ends
back into the fabric for about 1¹/₄in (3cm), then cut them off.
Now turn the work over and cut across the rows of string half-
way down and carefully remove the weaving from the card.
Finish off the ends by knotting them together in twos (and
one three), or by oversewing with matching thread, working
diagonally across two threads and down two as shown to
make a fringe. Trim the fringe to the length you require.

(right)
Design sheet **Glasshouses and
Greenhouses** by Carole
Waddle. Exploratory work on
dyed butter-muslin using
pulled threads and machine
embroidery. *16¹/₂ x 24in
(42 x 61cm)*

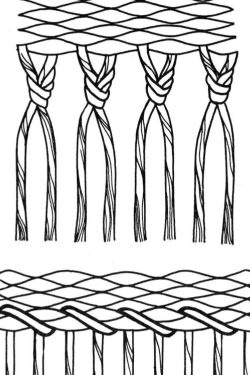

To finish off, knot or oversew a
matching fringe

Here are some exercises; please follow the above procedure for each.

a Work in one colour range only, but play with different textures and thicknesses of thread.

b Now work with two plain threads in different colours. Work across a third of your threads, turn, and weave back to the edge. Continue in this way until you have woven a strip, then weave a strip in your second colour, returning to the first colour for the third section. You will have produced three separate strips. Now weave a block of several rows across the full width to unite them and continue making your strips (perhaps reversing the colours) and your full width blocks until you have completed your piece of weaving.

c Use string for this and incorporate various 'found objects' across the weft, such as iris leaves, straw, grasses, etc, or some man-made materials such as silver paper, perspex, drinking-straws, etc, with rows of woven string.

d Try working part way across your warp, then returning and running a different thread from the other side. When you meet the first one, link them as shown in the diagram.

This is a tapestry weaving technique and offers much scope for blending colours and textures, for working from a design either abstract or figurative. When you have finished, and because you are an embroiderer, you can add extra stitches, French knots, beads, etc, to the surface, or you could add beads as you weave by threading your needle through them.

If you wish to explore this further, and on a larger scale, use the back of an old picture frame, or build a frame; it could be two or more metres tall! Knock nails into the top and bottom of the frame, about 1½cm apart, making sure they are in line with each other. Carry your warp threads up and down and round the nails and insert a flat stick or ruler before you begin weaving, to ensure adequate lengths of warp threads at each end for tying off and fringing.

Look at the tapestry *Eddy,* by Gill Davies (overleaf):

The wool for this tapestry woven face was handspun at a workshop in the Oman. The beautiful dark brown and cream colours made me want to do a black-white 'friendship' piece and initially I was going to depict two children holding hands. However, the scale proved to be too small and I changed my idea to a half-white/half-brown face.

Problems were solved as I went along by weaving then unpicking – not ideal, but the price one pays for not designing on paper first!

Eddy Grant had a song in the pop music charts at that time, so the dreadlocks were inspired by him and the name has stuck!

e Wrap a wire lampshade ring with tape or strips of fabric, working at an angle so that the edges overlap each other and cover the frame very tightly, then stitch the end neatly in position. Lay it on a table and place a curtain ring quite carefully within the circle, probably off-centre, then using a strong smooth thread of your colour scheme, and a sharp needle, stitch through the tape on the outer ring across to the curtain ring and back again. Continue doing this until the curtain ring is quite firmly held where you placed it, keeping your threads very taut. Consider whether these warp threads should be evenly spaced all round, or be arranged in blocks of varying sizes (see diagram).

Now, using a tapestry needle, weave across different sections using threads or fabric strips in a planned colour scheme, making good use of textural variety, and travelling

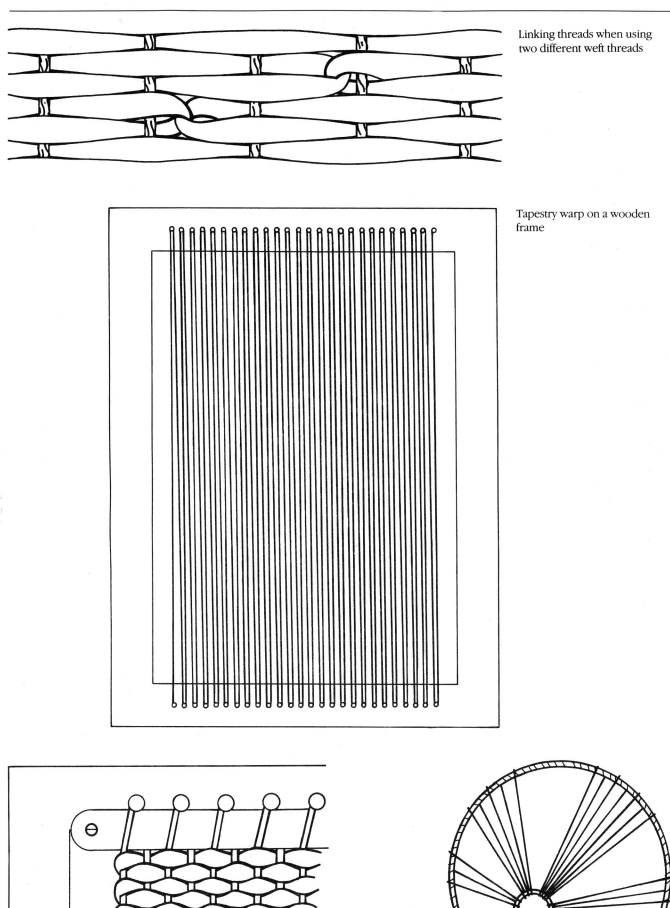

Linking threads when using two different weft threads

Tapestry warp on a wooden frame

Detail of tapestry weaving

Warp threads between two rings

from one group of warp threads to another to create a feeling of movement. When you have finished weaving you may choose to work round the rings with a buttonhole stitch. Make a loop at the top so it can hang, perhaps as a mobile.

Ruth Robbins worked in this way, using the bottom part of a wooden embroidery frame for her basic structure.

(The frame) was bound with thrums wool, then strung across with weaving cotton. Threads of varying thickness, rough, smooth, shiny, bouclé, were woven across the strung threads in groups tapering to a fine point near the centre where the threads crossed, an interesting focal point. Many of the weaving threads were unravelled from samples of furnishing fabric; very short lengths of lovely colours could be used, ranging from the darkest burgundy through all the reds, flames, oranges, cerise to palest shell-pink.

Woven Ring by Ruth Robbins, an example of experimental weaving. *14in (36cm) diameter*

Eddy by Gill Davies. A piece of tapestry weaving using handspun wool. *13 x 17in (33 x 43cm)*

Folding and cutting

Fabrics, like paper, can be folded and cut, then opened out, applied to a contrasting background and enriched with stitchery. It is advisable to use firm fabrics that do not fray too much, or back them with iron-on Vilene (fusible webbing), and do work on a scale large enough for the actual application to be manageable.

Fold a strip of fabric about 3in (8cm) deep into a zigzag and press the folds, then cut a V in one edge which would open as shown.

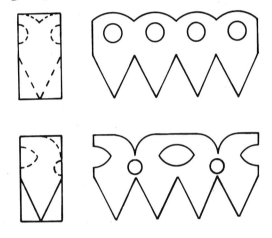

Fold it together again and make further cuts in one of two ways (see diagrams).

Another approach is to cut across the strip in some way and separate the pieces as here.

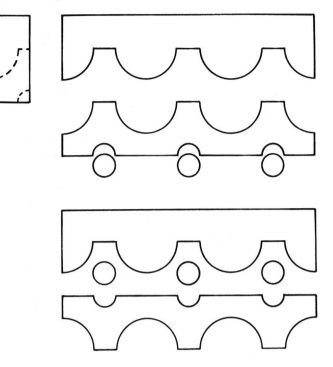

Build up a series of 'ribbons' in different colours and rearrange them until you are satisfied with the placing; try adding an odd circle, diamond shape, etc, that you have cut away, as well. Now stitch them all down using a close zigzag stitch on the sewing-machine, or by any other means that seems appropriate. Using actual ribbons could work well and transparent fabrics offer a wealth of potential, either overlaying each other, or in combination with more solid fabrics.

Other shapes can be cut and folded, such as a square or a circle. These can be folded into four or eight or more sections. Try to vary the sizes of the shapes you cut, contrasting large with small and perhaps grading from the centre to the edge.

The Hawaiian appliqué quilts exploit this method of designing most interestingly. In these, the cotton units are hand-applied and the edges turned under skilfully with the needle.

John Field Nocturne: paper-cut by Jill Bell-Scott

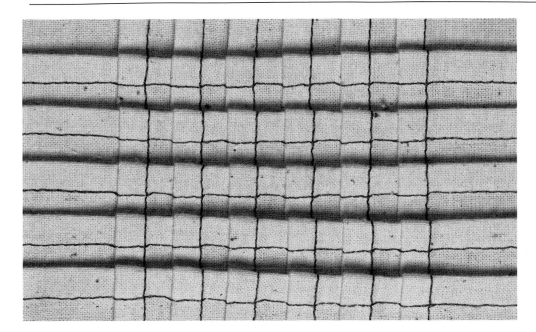

Tucks, machined to make a grid

Tucks, pressed and machined to one side then the other

Pleating and tucking

Pleats can be wide or narrow and face to left or right, or they can radiate. If cut on the bias they can be encouraged to curve when laid on a surface. They can be machined along the top edge to hang loosely, and grouped or draped on a vertical background.

Tiny pleats form the basis for smocking, which may be worked in a traditional manner, or quite freely; smocking on striped material can be very attractive. It might be interesting to change the scale quite radically and smock using cords on a heavy coating cloth, or on leather, perhaps punching holes and using eyelets.

Tucks can be machined across a fabric in one direction, and pressed, then more tucks machined across the first at right angles, to produce a grid. They can also be pressed to the right, and machined across to the right, then pressed to the left and machined in that direction; if the fabric is striped, that will give an interesting colour effect.

Try working tucks diagonally across striped fabrics. What else can you do with stripes?

Sheila Goldsworthy describes the experiments that led to her cushion *Shadows,* (overleaf):

In making a study on the theme 'Shadows', my interest in patchwork led me to experiment with ticking fabric.

Pleating the fabric created areas of light and dark caused by the grouping of the stripes. The resulting sculptural surface created more shadows within the pleats. The corrugated lines of red needlecord provided a striking contrast in texture to the ticking.

The ticking was pleated throughout the length and the pleats were then stitched flat down the length of the material. Subsequent rows of stitching followed taking a random course, each time pushing the pleats in the opposite direction. Experimental blocks of patches using the pleated fabric, unpleated shaped ticking and needlecord were made before I was satisfied with the final design for my cushion.

To accentuate the lines, couching in red and black cotton perlé was applied.

Tucks can be corded on the sewing-machine using a zipper foot. If the fabric is fine, like silk or organdie, the colour of cords could show through. Large tucks can be threaded with dowel rods or thin strips of card, or stuffed with wadding. Tucks need not be parallel or straight, of course.

A stiffened fabric such as calico interlined with Vilene (fusible webbing) begins to curl when tucked. If tucks are worked first on the front and the next section on the back, they will curl in opposite directions.

Calico Diamonds is an example of working in this way. The tucks varied in width and distance apart. Eventually the units were stiffened further, with a backing of buckram and lining of more calico. This idea has not yet been exhausted.

Changing the scale and the types of fabric selected can turn the ordinary into the unusual.

Shadows, a cushion by Sheila Goldworthy, combining the pleating of striped pillow–ticking with patchwork techniques to produce shadows

Steps to the Sea Note the similarity of shapes with **Calico Diamonds**

Calico Diamonds Tucks machined across stiffened calico cause the material to curl and produce a sculptural effect. *4 x 6ft (1.22 x 1.83m)*

Working into a grid

The grid has been a topic of much interest in recent years: It might be ready-made, such as a piece of rug-canvas or plastic fencing, or one constructed across a rectangular frame with strips of fabric, or thickish threads, sticks of bamboo, etc. A more delicate version could be worked into curtain net, either plain or more elaborate (another exercise from the 1970s). Alternatively the grid could be of gold threads laid on a mounted piece of Thai silk.

When the particular grid has been established, what then? Canvaswork stitches can be worked on an enlarged scale with suitably thick threads as in Elizabeth Ashurst's panel *Fields of Fire* on page 168.

Julia Burrowes also uses rug-canvas. She describes her wall-hanging *Hydrangeas* (overleaf):

> This technique, known in the North of England as tabby, proggy, stobby or clippy rugmaking, lends itself well to painterly effects, as it is possible to rework whole areas and rearrange the strips until the desired effect is achieved.
>
> For this reason the most suitable base is rug-canvas, as the more traditional hessian backing would be weakened by the removal and replacement of strips.
>
> The woollen cloth is hot-dyed to produce a thick felted fabric which will not fray and can be sculpted if desired. Dyeing with strong and weak solutions produces many tones of the same hue which are used to produce the effect of shading. Infinite variations of colour and tone can be used in each piece, as a 5 x 3ft rug contains an average of over two thousand fabric strips.
>
> Inspiration comes from many sources, sometimes from the colours themselves, sometimes from a particular scene, or a collection of shapes and forms.
>
> I do not find it necessary to plan out in detail before starting a rug, as this can prevent spontaneity. Instead I draw and make colour sketches, in order to immerse myself in the subject, and then work from instinct. This is far more time-consuming, but is extremely satisfying, often producing surprising and pleasing results.

Eirian Short's panel (overleaf) is not an example of working into a grid but, interestingly, it is another, quite different, interpretation of the same theme. This embroiderer set up a still life in the corner of her studio and worked from that. She likes to make her images as solid and real as possible and always stitches with crewel wool, which is fine enough to allow three or four threads to be used at one time, so enabling her to mix colours 'in the needle'.

For working into various types of grid, all sorts of alternative materials could be used, such as old tights (panty hose), torn strips of printed dress fabrics, plastic bags (both transparent and opaque), string and rope, and stitches could be carried out on a giant scale.

How can ribbons be used in relation to a grid? Again, they can be wide or narrow, plain or patterned, shiny or matt, and can be woven singly through a grid or in groups. They can be knotted, pleated, tied in bows or plaited.

Collect together all kinds of oddments, and try out your own ideas. Working on a large scale can be quite an adventure, and so can 'small and exquisite'.

Stacked Tables Note the grid pattern

(opposite)
Garden Trees, wall-hanging in black, grey and white felt by Jenny Cowern *4 x 5ft (122 x 153cm)*

Working with felt

Although its origins are uncertain, it is thought that felt is probably the oldest form of textile – in Persia its discovery was ascribed to the son of Solomon.

Felt-making today is something of a rediscovered craft and many people working in embroidery are experimenting in this area. Felt has several qualities that differentiate it from other fabrics; it can be quite thick, it is non-fraying and you can make it yourself (see Bibliography for books on felt-making).

In making felt it is possible to create areas of solid colour, grading gently from one to another, to add wisps of colour here and there, and also to incorporate threads. Areas from one piece of felt can be cut and applied in another to produce clear-cut shapes with hard edges. Large designs can be created which are complete in themselves, as in Jenny Cowern's wall-hanging *Garden Trees,* but embroiderers are likely to work into their felt with stitchery, to add contrasting fabrics, beads, etc, or to layer it in different ways. Working on felt with a sewing-machine will produce a quilted effect.

The thickness of handmade felt is useful in layering. Shapes

Hydrangeas by Eirian Short. A panel based on a still life drawing and worked in French knots with crewel wool in colours 'mixed in the needle'. *20in (51cm) square*

can be built up on top of each other, while elsewhere the felt can be cut through to reveal layers below, perhaps of several different colours, as in the panel *Harlequin* (page 82). This began by my chancing to find the large diamond-shaped plastic sequins in black and white. This led to the idea of exploring diamond shapes by working with several layers of felt. The first layer was the red, superimposed with black and then with the darker grey which became the surface area. The different layers were cut and folded back in the central unit. The pale grey and white felt shapes were added on top, as were the sequins.

If felt units are machined down just within the shapes, the edges will turn up a little and cast a slight shadow, so there is also the possibility of working in a self-colour.

Not everyone will be making their own felt and there is plenty of scope in using the bought kind. Try cutting or plaiting it, or making rolls that are short and fat, or long and thin,

Hydrangeas by Julia Burrowes. An example of working into a grid. *38 x 55in (96 x 140cm)*

Swiss Flowers

and attaching them on their sides or standing up on end. Try pleating and tucking – what else can you think of? Susan Hodgson has been very inventive in this way in her sampler (overleaf).

Working with patterned fabrics
We are accustomed to seeing patterned fabrics used in different kinds of patchwork. They add a special quality and richness to the work, as well as a feeling for history as styles and patterns change.

Can we use these fabrics in different contexts and achieve something unobtainable by other means?

Take, for example, a floral dress fabric and examine it carefully; it might suggest possibilities for enrichment and for changing its emphasis. You might choose to quilt round some of the shapes with a sewing-machine, adding stitchery or some spray-painting. Leaves or flowers could be cut out of a spare piece of the fabric, stiffened with iron-on Vilene (fusible webbing), and reapplied either flat, or standing away from the surface. Alternatively you could assemble units from a number of different fabrics which need not be floral; patterns varying in scale might be used together.

Checked gingham was used in schools at one time as a base in which small geometric patterns were stitched. Certainly the possibilities were there, but those sad mauve crosses on green gingham aprons must have bored children utterly. In New Zealand recently I saw an up-dated version of this (imported from the USA) called, curiously enough, 'Chicken Scratch', in which rich and varied patterns are worked into small scale gingham.

Heavy corduroy fabrics have simple or more complex stripes inherent in their construction. These can be cut and used with the stripes lying in different directions, so that the light falls interestingly on the pile, giving great richness.

Some patterned fabrics might awaken memories of something you have seen or experienced. It might be interesting to build up a three-dimensional scene inside a fairly large, shallow box standing on its end or side, rather like a stage-setting. Fabrics could be bunched up, or rolled, frayed, etc, and padded or supported on chicken wire and pieces of cardboard. It might depict a carnival, a grotto, or tomatoes growing in the greenhouse! Having conceived your idea you could research your subject-matter further, but the idea will have come from the initial handling of materials.

A patterned fabric might be used as a background for, say, a piece of machine embroidery, because it evokes the feeling and atmosphere you wish to capture. Barbara Siedlecka makes use of patterned materials to produce a rich texture in her panel *A Sampler of Rhodes* (page 109).

In working directly and freely with fabrics, take care to avoid dropping a shapeless splodge of silk on a background and calling it a gardenia. That is an avoidance tactic – it is not exploring with an open mind, but rather a pointless pursuit of an end result and therefore cheating!

Punk in a Garden, painted
paper figures in a box by
Charlotte Lees *11 x 13 x 4in
(28 x 33 x 10cm)*

Wrapping and piping

Wrapping materials of various kinds with fabrics and threads offers broad extensions to the scope of embroidery and is to be seen in the work of embroiderers and fibre artists such as Tadek Beutlich.

Strips of wood, shaped pieces of cardboard or polystyrene, cotton reels, match-boxes, or rolls of card from kitchen or toilet rolls can be covered and wrapped with fabrics, ribbons, old tights (panty hose), silk or metal threads, etc.

Piping strips can be made, using bias-cut fabrics wrapped over piping cord or rope, and applied to a background. Diana Springall does this in her *Book of Kells* panel, an interesting example of an artist evolving a mode of expression that exactly matches her ideas.

The work was commissioned by an Irish family and the subject was their suggestion. I looked at a good

Felt sampler by Susan Hodgson. *9in (23cm) square*

Harlequin An exploration of the diamond shape by cutting down through layers of felt or building up above the surface level. The black and white sequins initiated the idea. *24 x 34in (61 x 86cm)*

reproduction of the *Book of Kells* and had to decide whether the colour, the pattern or the line was more important. Because of the variety of descriptive subjects contained in the pages I felt that Line was going to give greatest expression – to keep the birds, snakes, fishes, etc, visible.

Flat lines would perhaps be dull, so I raised them by means of piping cord into a low relief. The one-colour dupion was chosen in consultation with the client in order to be the centre-piece of their new living-room.

If you decide to experiment with working in this way, in the present context of working directly from materials, perhaps you should make the piping strips first and see how you can use them in an inventive way.

Rolls of felt, thick card or other materials can be covered with fabrics and wrapped here and there with threads, or criss-crossed with ribbons, or bound totally with threads of varying texture. Hannah Frew Paterson has made a feature of wrapping, to be seen in her panel *Tex-Tech* (overleaf):

Man-made mechanical objects have been a continuing source of inspiration for one aspect of my work.

Tex-Tech is one of a series of designs based on the patterns and complexities of printed circuit boards. Elements from these boards were selected as units of design to contrast with the repeating parallel lines. Initially, these were manipulated in paper form to establish the basic composition. After experimenting with various materials the units were produced by rolling small rectangles of metallic leather round a knitting needle to form tubes, which in turn were wrapped with tiny pieces of brightly-coloured silk fabric fringed at the edges and over-wrapped with shiny silk and rayon threads to highlight their 3D quality. They were attached to the background fabric by the use of fuse-wire threaded through heavy gold purl. The repeating lines of the circuits were produced using conventional laid goldwork on top of very narrow strips of metallic leather.

Some people make frames for their embroidery by wrapping threads closely round a card mount, keeping them in place as they work with double-sided tape stuck on the back of the card – see Chapter 7, 'Presentation'.

Wrapped units can be assembled on a background or suspended as a mobile, perhaps combined with cords and tassels, beads, etc, or built together into a piece of free standing soft sculpture. See also the panel *Squares and Stripes* by Constance Howard on page 6.

Using transparent fabrics
Exercise 12 of Chapter 1 suggests experimenting with net to discover how interesting and subtle variations in colour can

Book of Kells by Diana Springall. This is a detail of a panel *6 x 2ft (183 x 61cm)*, worked in self–coloured dupion using piping-cord to raise the lines

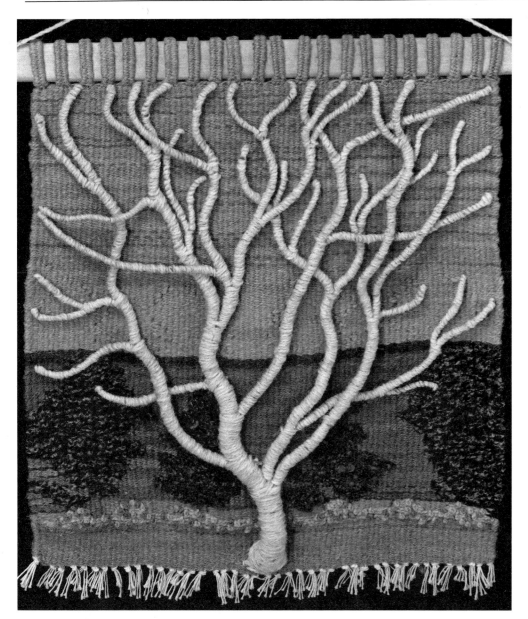

Tree by Isabel del Strother, an example of wrapping applied to a tapestry

be achieved by overlaying several cut or torn pieces of fine fabric in one colour or in several. These effects can be enhanced by stitching underneath as well as on top of the materials; alternatively fabrics can be ruched or tucked.

Today there are many beautiful sheer fabrics available, such as organzas, some with an iridescent quality which might be combined with lurex fabrics, gold or silver kid, silk or metal threads (stitched or floating) and machine embroidery to give a feeling of magic, luxury or delicacy. See, for example, Judith Smalley's wall-hanging *Amethyst* and Rosemary Jarvis's piece *Fanfare* (overleaf).

Judith Smalley writes:

> The design *Amethyst* originated from a study of a section of amethyst quartz. I took a very small area from which the basic motif was derived, which was then enlarged to a variety of sizes on a photocopier. From these I eventually built up the design of the final hanging as a line drawing.
>
> The use of fabric is always a very important part of my work and I especially enjoy using shot and transparent fabric because of their colour-mixing qualities. For this piece they seemed particularly appropriate as it was the translucency of the amethysts and the colours of the stone which had attracted me.
>
> The fabrics were applied by bonding and with bands of free machining worked over them – running stitch and silk paint were used to echo the design.

Rosemary Jarvis writes of *Fanfare:*

> This small panel is a combination of my love of colour, a fascination with metal threadwork and the special quality and feel of silk threads and fabrics. The starting point was the riot of vibrant colours of the flowers in a hanging-basket. The background is dyed silk, backed with calico, with various gold braids and strips of leather couched down by hand and machine. The border is made from torn strips of dyed silk, worked with running stitches in silk thread. I wanted to express real joy in the combination of intense colour with gold, and a feeling of 'life' in this exploration of the qualities of large-scale *or nué* combined with random-dyed and painted silk.

Such exquisite fabrics may not, of course, be appropriate to certain pieces of work. In *Silent Forest* (page 33) where trees are dying for lack of space and daylight, lovely shimmering fabrics would be quite out of place.

Amethyst by Judith Smalley, using shot and transparent fabrics. *24 x 41¹/₂in (61 x 105cm)*

Fanfare by Rosemary Jarvis. Work with dyed silks and metal threads in response to vibrant colours of flowers in a hanging-basket. *8 x 11in (20 x 28cm)*

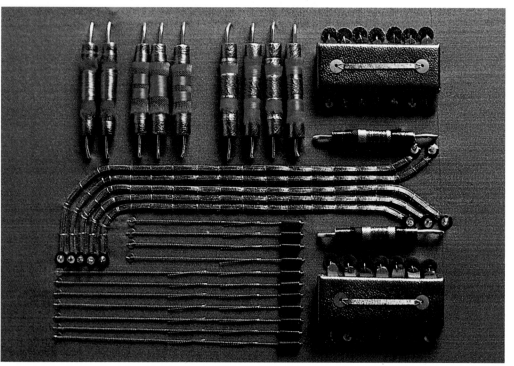

Tex-Tech by Hannah Frew Paterson. An example of wrapping, using silk fabrics and threads on rolled metallic leather in a design based on the pattern of a printed circuit board. *10 x 12in (25 x 31cm)*

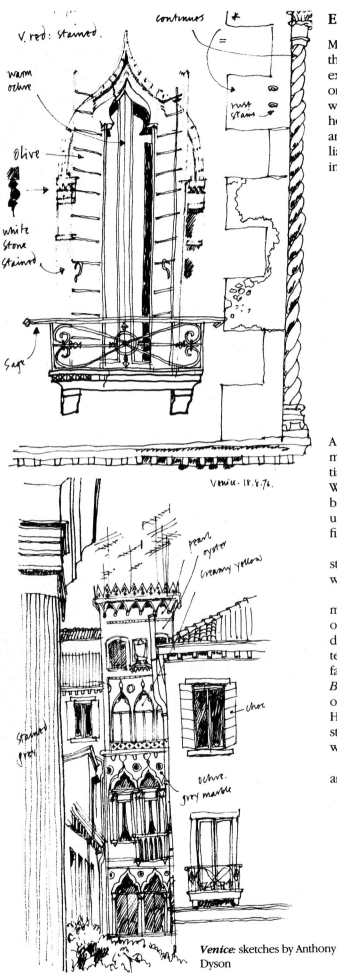

V. red: stained.

warm ochre

olive

white stone stained

Sage

continues

rust stains

Venice · 18.8.76.

pearl oyster
creamy yellow

choc

stained grey

ochre.
grey marble

Venice: sketches by Anthony Dyson

EXPLORING GEOMETRIC FORM

Many people think of geometry as an academic subject of their schooldays, without much bearing on their subsequent experiences; others come to embroidery with a mathematical or scientific background and may enjoy the challenge of working from this starting point, as did Margaret Pascoe in her panel *Rugby Football* (overleaf). This was a response to an advertisement for Gulf Oil which showed blocks of brilliant contrasting colours gradually increasing and decreasing in size, in a way which produced a three-dimensional effect.

I hoped to reproduce this effect in embroidery and experimented with small samples. As usual the materials used, tapestry wools, perlé threads and the canvas, took over and dictated what was or was not possible.

All stitches were worked on the diagonal, with blocks of 2 stitches over 2 threads, 3 over 3 threads and so on until a block of 10 stitches over 10 threads was made; each stitch started from the centre line with further blocks added until all the stitches had been repeated as in the diagram, and a Rugby football shape appeared. When blocks overlapped, adjustments had to be made.

Graduating shades of blue and green were used and empty shapes between the satin stitches were filled with tent stitch in gold perlé. A background of crewel wool in a gobelin stitch was added.

A geometric structure underlies many aspects of our environment, eg, paving stones, a table, a box of stationery are essentially based on the vertical, the horizontal and the right angle. Wheels, tunnels, drain-pipes, clocks and gothic arches are based on the circle. In nature too we find geometric structure underlying the form in brain coral, the honeycomb, a star fish, and the symmetry of a beetle.

The warp and weft in weaving are of vertical and horizontal structure and many weaving designs make use of stripes in warp and weft; Scottish tartans are an example of this.

The geometric structure of fabric invites counted thread methods in embroidery, worked on an evenweave fabric, ie, one in which warp and weft threads are alike in thickness and distance apart. In blackwork, tiny repeating motifs and patterns are achieved by counting the threads of the background fabrics (see 'Tone Value', Chapter 5 and Gill Pickup's panel *Black for Gold*, page 172). Pattern darning and cross stitch are other such methods, and drawn and pulled threadwork, and Hardanger also depend on counting, while canvas work stitches are essentially geometric in construction and are worked into a canvas grid.

Caroline Baker's panel *Urban Colours* (overleaf) is another example of this method:

I rarely begin a canvas work with a fixed image in mind, as I like a piece to take on its own identity. If it is working, it will tell me what is needed. Inspiration flows from colour.

The simple overstitch allows me to exploit the delights of colour rather than complex stitchery which would detract from it and hinder my instinctive method of working. I spend hours looking at the work, holding wools against it until the combination looks right.

The final outcome is very pleasing. For me it clearly represents 'urban colours', due to its tonal

Wesolych by Barbara Siedlecka

range and geometric form, columns of colour illustrating a sympathetic landscape of urban architecture, although it started life as a piece encompassing the colours of the sea.

In contrast, the sampler worked by Victor Fa makes use of changes in stitch, texture and scale which gain strength by being worked in off white threads only.

Patchwork, of course, is traditionally constructed on geometric bases, such as a square, rectangle, triangle, hexagon, etc, and very elaborate and complex looking designs are a result of clever, yet simple mathematical thinking.

While working in an Art studio adjacent to the Maths Department at a College of Education, I was persuaded to explore the possibilities of designing using units such as

Canvas work sampler by Victor Fa, which contrasts the scale and textures of stitches, without the use of colour

Rugby Football by Margaret Pascoe. The embroiderer has evolved a system of the sizes of canvas stitch blocks to create a three-dimensional effect.
7 x 12in (18 x 30cm)

90

circles only, or crosses, diamonds (see *Harlequin,* page 83), squares and triangles. Various methods were used including goldwork, fabric collage and stitchery, layering in felt, and machine embroidery combined with transparent fabrics. Tessellation also offers interesting possibilities.

So, how can we make use of geometric form as source material for embroidery design?

Geometry in the environment

Search the man-made and the natural environment for forms with an underlying geometric structure. This could be a school or local project involving an outing to a water-mill, the geological museum or to watch a potter or weaver at work; what does your locality offer? Make a record by sketching or taking photographs as for any primary source of inspiration.

Urban Colours by Caroline Baker. Using one simple stitch focusses upon the embroiderer's love of colour. *18 x 19in (46 x 48cm)*

91

Geometry in ornament

Look at Gothic or Saracenic architecture, or other forms of geometric ornament either at the library or, better still, on a visit to a museum. Make a record of something you especially like, placing a special emphasis on the geometric aspects, and later develop this for your own purposes.

Counted methods of embroidery

Take a piece of single-thread canvas, about 13 threads to the inch (2.5cm), and collect threads of a thickness which will nicely cover the canvas without distorting it, in a variety of colours and textures. To prevent the work from pulling out of shape, mount the canvas in a ring-frame, or on an old picture frame with drawing-pins (thumbtacks), making sure it is square and taut. Use a tapestry needle of suitable size; this will have a blunt point and so avoid splitting the stitches. Lean the frame on the edge of the table if possible, so you can work with one hand on top and the other underneath the canvas.

Choose a stitch which fits into a square, such as flat stitch or chequer stitch. **Flat stitch** is worked diagonally over 1, 2, 3, 2, 1 threads of canvas, each block in the opposite direction from the previous one. **Chequer stitch** is worked diagonally over 1, 2, 3, 4, 3, 2, 1 threads of canvas, with alternate blocks filled in with tent stitches.

a Work an area of your chosen stitch using one thread only.
b Now work another area in which you vary the tones and textures of the threads, but in one colour only.
c Now try varying the sizes of your blocks in quite a free way, changing your tones and textures as in b).
d Now see if you can achieve a feeling of movement, by varying the size of the blocks and the colours, tones and textures of your threads.

People sometimes assume that work based on the structure of canvas or evenweave fabric demands a geometric type of design and so produce rather stiff squarish figures or animals, or choose buildings because of their vertical, horizontal and oblique forms. This is not necessarily so and, while canvas stitches are essentially based on a grid structure, designs in which they are used can be made to flow quite freely. Florentine stitch also offers an interesting example of this, even when used in a traditional manner.

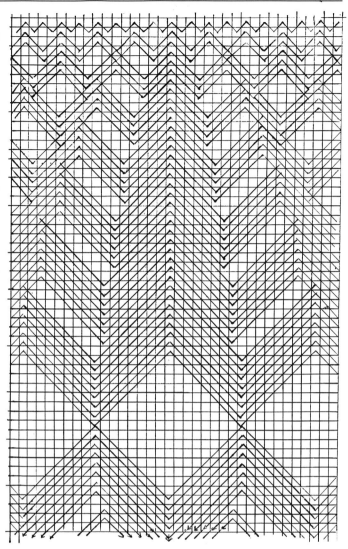

Rugby Football, diagram by Margaret Pascoe

(left) Flat stitch
(right) Chequer stitch

(overleaf)
Rug by Valerie Tulloch. An example of strip patchwork using fabrics saved from coats, skirts, etc, some of which were over-dyed in the washing-machine to relate them to each other. *47 x 77in (1.20 x 1.96m)*

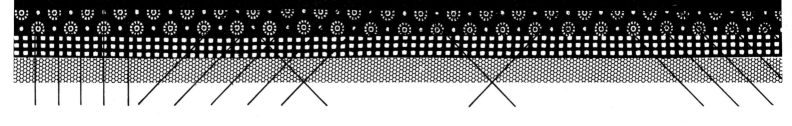

The joined strip with cutting
lines marked

Moving one unit up and one
down

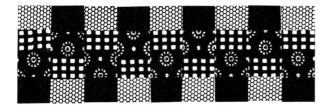

Reversing alternate units

Using triangular
pieces

Stepping the units down and
adding a diagonal strip

Strip patchwork

Collect four cotton fabrics which look well together, eg, one dark, one patterned, one light and one bright, and tear off a strip of each, about 1¼in (3cm) wide, across the full width of the fabric, ie, about 36in (92cm) or more in length. When you have selected the best sequence for the strips, join them together very accurately on the sewing-machine and press the seams together, to lie under the darker strips in each case. Tear an extra strip of each colour.

Mark your fabrics using ruler and set square and a sharp black or white pencil, then cut the units carefully.

a Cut a set of vertical units about 1¼in (3cm) wide.

b Cut a set of units at 45°.

c Cut a set of triangles at 45°.

d Cut a set of units at 45°, but in the opposite direction from b). Now place your vertical units side by side, but try out a number of placings, such as

a Moving one up and one down.

b Reversing alternate ones and perhaps inserting some of your plain strips between the units.

c Stepping them down and running one or more of your plain strips diagonally across the zigzag edge.

When you have some arrangements you like, machine the pieces together neatly and press the two edges together under the darker fabric.

d Now investigate the oblique units in similar ways.

e What can you do with the triangular pieces?

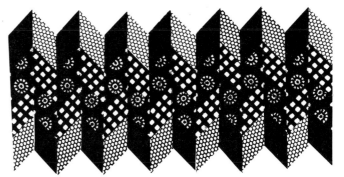

Exploring oblique units

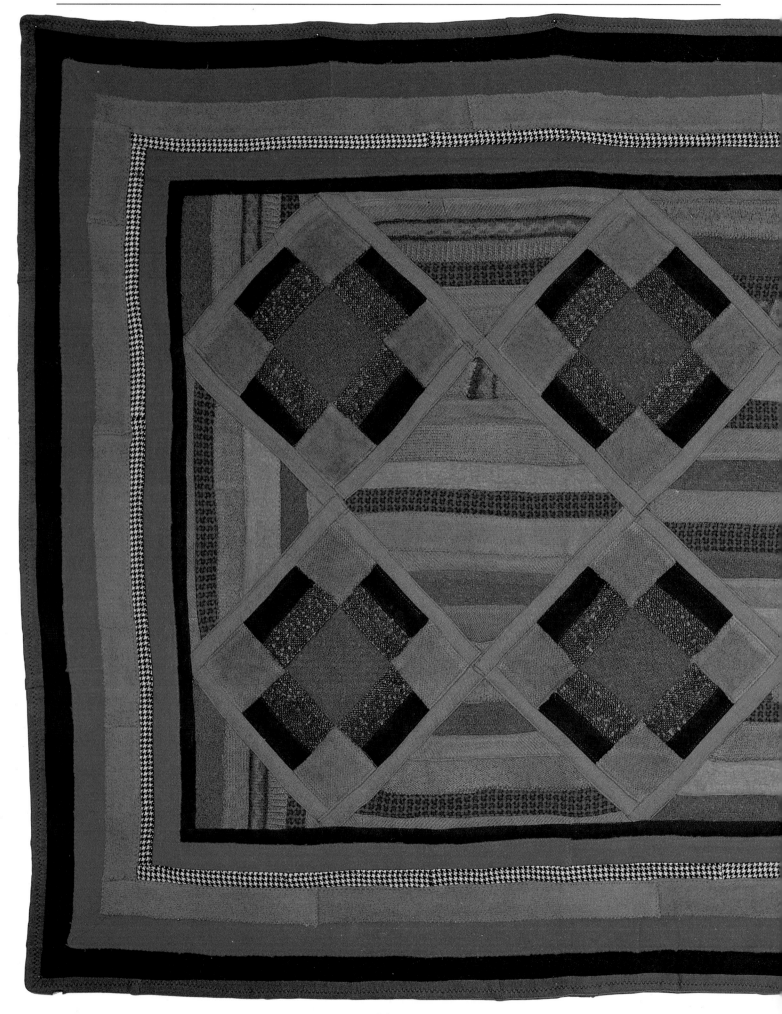

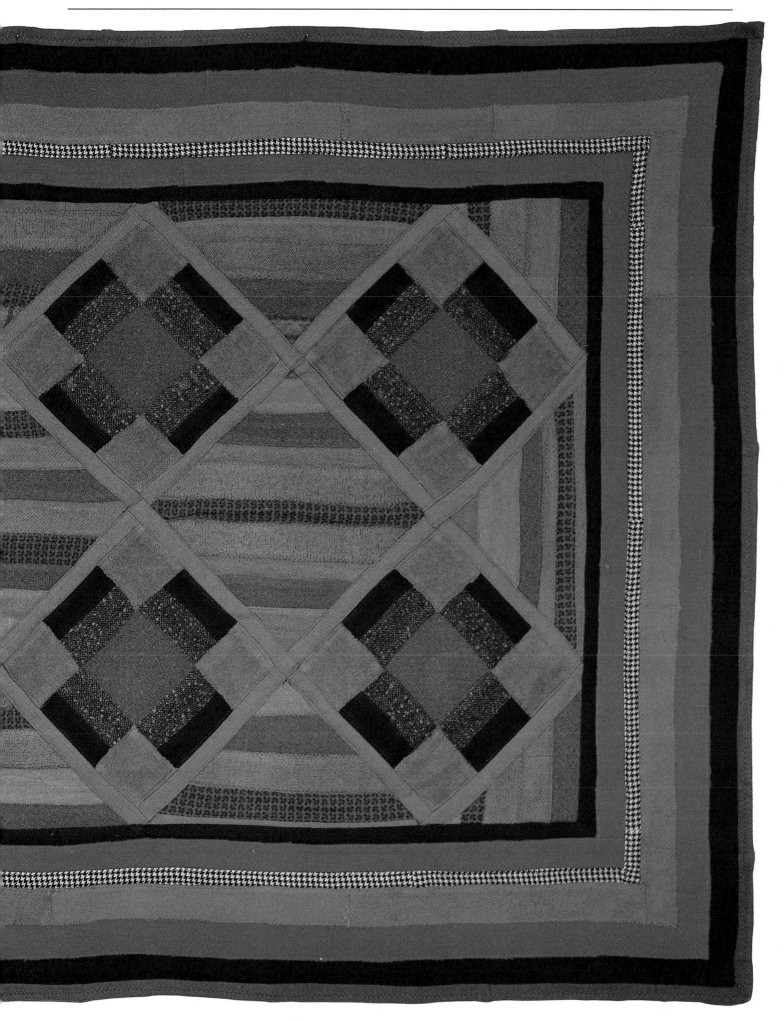

Later you could make some long strips consisting of a greater number of fabrics, or you could vary the widths or the angles of cutting, or work through a smooth transition of tones in one colour. You could make two long strips in colour schemes that harmonise and interrelate units from each. What happens if you cut a lot of vertical units, each slightly wider than the last? Take care to keep these in sequence!

Why not design a cushion cover, incorporating the different types of units, or a waistcoat, a bag, the hem of a skirt, a large wall-hanging? Would you change the scale of the units for any of these?

Do not forget to mount your samplers.

Valerie Tulloch describes her patchwork *Rug*:

> To re-use sheep's 'Rug' wool from home-made wartime quilts I produced a series of machine-patchwork quilts using variations of a block pattern. Then when newly independent daughters needed rugs for bare floors the patchwork idea logically developed to utilise woollen material saved from coats, skirts, pullovers and dressmaking off-cuts.
>
> For this rug, squares, rectangles and strips of fabric were machined on to cotton squares to form the basic repeating blocks, diamonds and triangles. Some fabrics were in acceptable colours, the rest were made to relate to each other by over-dyeing them together in the washing machine. Turquoise and purplish pink became transformed, though still recognisable, after treatment with less obtrusive colour (a common brownish dye).
>
> Individual blocks were machined to a base of old linen with lattice outlines and strip borders. Zigzag and straight stitches were used, the final border being taken over the edge to the back.

Joan Hobson describes her patchwork *Greenpeace*:

> I wanted to do a quilt in plain materials using a simple 3in block without a geometric pattern, relying on colour and texture to give interest.
>
> By dyeing and re-dyeing my original materials, and blending the centre strip of each block with the outer strip of the next, the colour-change could be subtle or dramatic.
>
> Choosing green as my basic colour and working right from yellow through to blue, with some undertones of red, I could use all the variety of colour in land and seascapes.

After eighteen months' 'work' what could be more appropriate than to give my Green Piece to support the cause I think fundamental to the well-being of future generations, namely, Greenpeace?

Design with a geometry kit

Another interesting way to start designing is by using a simple geometry kit consisting of a ruler, compass, set squares (both 45° and 30°/60°) and some well-sharpened H or HB pencils, a biro (ballpoint) and some sheets of plain paper, size A4.

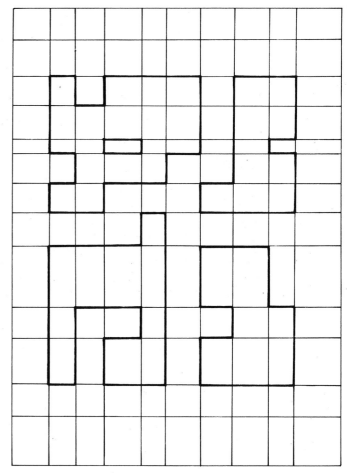

(above) Design using geometry kit
(below) Design repeated

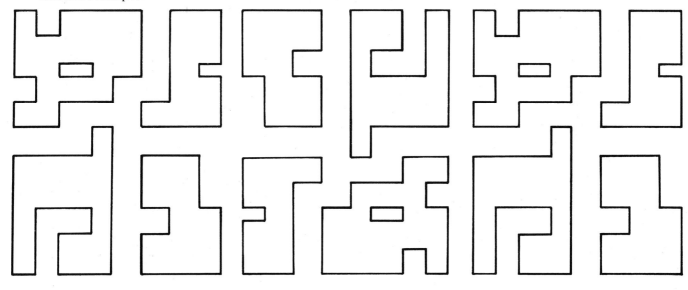

a   Start by drawing lines right across the paper, both horizontally and vertically, varying in distance apart. Now, select some of the lines that create a pattern and ink them in, using biro (ballpoint) and ruler.

b   Experiment on a fresh sheet using verticals and horizontals and adding oblique lines, either at 45° or at 30°/60°, but not both, as all these angles together could cause visual confusion! Ink in your chosen lines.

c   What can you do with a compass, by varying the sizes of circles or arcs of circles, and by overlapping them? Again, ink in the best lines.

d   Work out a pattern within a 25cm square and consider how it could be repeated: side by side, in mirror image, etc.

Greenpeace by Joan Hobson. A detail of a quilt using *3in (7.5cm)* blocks, so that the centre strip of each blends with the outer strip of the next. *8ft (2.44m) square*

Try colouring your different designs. Now, look at them carefully and consider different ways in which you might use them. How would they look in overlapping layers of silk organzas, or quilted in calico? Would any enlarge successfully, or could you repeat them in some way as a design for a patchwork quilt?

Pencil sketches from the
Dancers series

WORKING FROM IDEAS

The starting points we have considered so far have arisen either from personal observation, or from working directly with fabrics and threads, or other materials.

There is another type of approach wherein an individual or a group may seize upon an idea, which could come from social events, literature, the locality, etc, the possibilities seem limitless. Having settled upon the idea, it will then be necessary to proceed with a design in the usual way, either by finding visual reference material, or by making studies or sketches, developing these further and translating them into the medium of fabrics and threads.

Working from a theme
A theme is an important idea or topic, perhaps less specific or tangible than 'subject', that can lead to the making of a series

After the Dancing Class A piece on the theme of 'Figures in movement', using some applied fabrics and long straight stitches in black, greys and white silk threads.
12¹/₂ x 17in (32 x 43cm)

of images. Such a theme may come very much from the heart and might be in support of 'Women's Lib', 'Save our Trees', or other social issues of the day, or develop from, say, a fascination for reptiles, or from a remembered dream. Themes I have seen pursued in embroidery include 'Connections', 'Hearts', 'Notting Hill Carnival' and 'Rock Crystals' (see Gillian Harvey's work, page 133). A personal theme is 'Figures in Movement', such as dancers and children at play eg, *After the Dancing Class*.

The idea came about some years ago after taking black and white photographs of dancers using a fast film but, by mistake, a slow speed. The blurred images which resulted were very exciting and many drawings followed; they have developed into a series of twenty-one to date, including *Boy with Two Ice Creams* (overleaf). I work mainly on silk noile stretched on a frame, 'drawing' with long straight stitches, usually in black and white, and perhaps using fabric collage, spray-painting, machine embroidery and, on one occasion, first printing a lithograph on the fabric.

Such themes may involve responding to, or participating in, some special experiences, or doing research, perhaps in a museum, laboratory, zoo, etc, and will probably lead to drawing, painting or taking photographs.

Imaginative response to a verbal description
Marian Richardson, an Art educator in the 1930s, pioneered her 'Shut Eye' method of inspiring work from her pupils. She would ask them to sit with their eyes shut as she described an incident from her own experience, such as a visit to the ballet. The pupils would then respond with drawings and paintings of their own and some most remarkable work emerged from this method of teaching.

Male Dancer, spray-painted and hand stitched. *9¹/₂ x 12¹/₂in (24 x 32cm)*

(opposite)
Boy with Two Ice Creams

What use can you make of this interesting idea, either for your own work, or to motivate other people? The essence must surely be a sincere expression of genuine feeling about something you saw or did. It does not have to be either beautiful or extraordinarily unusual, but it does need to have a ring of truth and to strike a chord of familiarity for your listener.

What sort of story or description can you produce from your own experience that will suggest some interesting images? Perhaps something urban – the hustle and bustle of the weekend shopping, a traffic jam, the school playground? Or how about something spooky – suddenly feeling all alone in a dark alley-way and hearing the sound of your own feet clattering hastily along the pavement? It could be something gentle and relaxing or a sudden bad storm; where were you, and what did it feel like?

Evocative titles, too, will often spark off a quick response, such as 'Thunder clouds over the hills', or 'Street-lights in the November fog', because they draw on experiences that many people have had at some time.

Drawings, paintings and sketches are likely to be the outcome of this type of work, perhaps using some kind of exaggeration to emphasise the special imaginative way of thinking.

The group project

Sometimes a group of people feel they would like to work together in some way and a joint project can offer a very rewarding experience. The Quilting Bee, the Friendship patchwork quilt, or the canvaswork wall-hanging for a local building have all offered scope for social as well as artistic pleasure. The question soon arises 'What shall we do?' and a search begins for a topic appropriate for and relevant to that particular group.

Winter Trees

The Kingston and District Branch of the Embroiderers' Guild recently completed a set of four large panels for Guildhall II, Kingston-upon-Thames, which show buildings in different areas of the Borough. Two of these are illustrated (overleaf). The project was designed and organised by two members, one of whom took many photographs of buildings from a list agreed with the Council. People then chose the ones they wished to embroider. Instruction sheets were issued regarding the size of the buildings and, in order to achieve unity, people were asked not to use perspective, but to take a flat-on front view. Tracings and photocopies were made which could be enlarged to the required size, giving guidelines for the proportions.

The buildings were worked in crewel wools in a limited range of colours on canvas of 14 or 16 threads to the inch (2.5cm) except for the windows, for which stranded cotton was used to give the effect of sheen and reflection. The trees were machine embroidered on net or water-soluble material. The materials were distributed in 'kits' but people could add touches of other colours and threads if necessary.

The background fabric of beige evenweave cotton, chosen to match the walls in the Guildhall, was mounted on a heavyweight calico and stretched on four wooden frames. Eventually the two organisers spent many hours arranging and rearranging the stitched buildings and machine embroidered greenery until they arrived at a satisfactory layout. Bronze kid was used for the lettering, padded with felt and stitched by Lydia Taylor. Over half the Branch members participated in the embroidery and many joined the four working parties held in members' homes for making up the panels.

Another group project might be a study of the history, geography and landscape of a stretch of your nearby river. This could involve the local community, both adults and children. A riverside walk in spring could include the examination of early flowers, the buds on the trees, a visit to a local farm, and the question of why the path was there and who walked along it in the past? There is plenty of subject matter for an embroidery, either on an individual basis or as a joint effort to make a wall-panel for the Village Hall.

SOURCES OF INSPIRATION – SUMMARY

You have made 'preparation' in terms of the theories of creativity, you have collected source material of various kinds and gathered together a number of sketches, photographs and samples of practical explorations, etc. You should feel ready and confident to move on to the next stage of translating an idea into a design.

But what if you still feel you do not know what to do, which idea to pursue or what means or methods of expression to use? Do not worry, this is not uncommon. In terms of creative response, you now drop your ideas into your subconscious for a while. This is the stage of creativity termed 'incubation'. Perhaps while looking back through the collected source material, or climbing a hill, you will suddenly pause – and then comes 'illumination' and you will know what you want to do with your ideas.

Wild Flowers by Stephen Lees

Kingston Panel: Kingston-upon-Thames 2ft 3in x 6ft (68.5 x 182cm)

***Kingston Panel: Chessington,
Tolworth, Surbiton** 2ft 3in x 6ft
(68.5 x 182cm)*. Two of the
four panels undertaken as a
group project by the Kingston
and District Branch of the
Embroiderers' Guild. The
buildings in canvas work and
the trees in machine
embroidery are applied to the
background fabric. Designed
and organised by Margaret
Rivers and Margaret Humphrey

CHAPTER 3

DEVELOPING A DESIGN AND CHOOSING A METHOD

Having found a source of inspiration, the next stage is to translate your sketches, photographs, samplers, etc which resulted from the various approaches discussed in Chapter 2 into a design for embroidery.

We shall also consider the importance that stitchery and different methods or means of working will have on the ensuing work; you may already feel inspired to move in a particular direction. This will involve decisions regarding the scale of working and of technical preparations to be made. Some methods currently of special interest are included in this section.

WORKING FROM DRAWINGS, SKETCHES OR PHOTOGRAPHS

In the records made of things observed, such as natural or man-made form, or work in a museum or art gallery, you are already likely to have translated something three-dimensional into two-dimensional form on your pieces of paper. Look at your drawings or photographs carefully and ask yourself what aspects interested you particularly. Perhaps your drawing has been very factual and accurate, but there may be certain qualities you wish to emphasise as you begin to design from the information before you. In all likelihood, however, either consciously or intuitively you will have put emphasis on the aspect which first captured your attention.

Designing is a process of selecting and rejecting, simplifying to exclude irrelevant detail and relating parts to each other and to the whole. Suppose you have observed that certain shapes seem to complement or echo each other, or that there is an underlying movement or rhythm that you would like to make a special feature in your design, then you would try out different ways of capturing these effects. Layout pads are useful in that they contain thin paper, adequate to draw and paint on, but thin enough to lay over a drawing or painting and see the lines and forms through it. Using one of these you can try out a series of ideas, or you may make gradual changes until you arrive at a final solution, as did Barbara Siedlecka for her panel *A Sampler of Rhodes* overleaf.

The colours I use tend to be cold and restrained but after a visit to Rhodes in mid-August I was influenced by the heat, pattern, texture and colour in the old town. Many drawings organised round a central square developed into *A Sampler of Rhodes,* which was a breakthrough for me in the use of sumptuous metallic and patterned fabrics and sizzling hot colour. The result was a composite picture of views through arches into courtyards, deep shade contrasting with pools of bright sunlight. Old and new, plain and patterned fabrics were used; the light bouncing off metallic threads and being absorbed by the variety of velvets and suedes created the atmosphere of place and time.

Sketches for *A Sampler of Rhodes* by Barbara Siedlecka

The Morvil Foxes by Eirian
Short

A Sampler of Rhodes by Barbara Siedlecka. This is a detail *23 x 28in (58 x 71cm)* of a panel *36in (91cm) square*. It is a composite picture of views through arches and courtyards designed from preliminary sketches

Building up a collage of tissue paper, or scraps torn from magazines or colour supplements, might be a useful way to work, adding paint here or there as you think fit. Keep all your sketches, roughs, design developments, etc, because you may decide to enlarge your intentions into a series of embroideries on the same theme.

Soon you will need to get a feeling of how this design could best be translated into embroidery. This may not happen at once; perhaps you will need a period of 'incubation'. Alternatively you may have known from the start how you would use your source material. Perhaps you have a favourite method, such as goldwork or canvaswork, and were searching for an idea you could use in this way, so your eye was drawn to subject matter which offered just the right textural or other formal qualities that would work well in that medium. Some methods demand considerable simplification from the original picture, for instance, a naturalistic representation would be very difficult and indeed quite inappropriate in quilting or canvas work.

When considering possible methods in which to develop your design, the question of scale is a matter for immediate consideration. Do you visualise making a large wall-hanging or a tiny, richly-stitched picture? Will you use a traditional embroidery method adapted, of course, to your needs, or will you work in mixed media, eg combining some method of printing, spray-painting or using fabric dyes, etc, with embroidery? Will you use padding, or work three-dimensionally?

Some years ago people would sometimes take the same design and carry it out in two or three different methods. The necessary adaptation of the design can be very interesting: the size and scale need to be varied for different methods, as in the two versions of a sea-urchin shell illustrated overleaf. *Sea Urchins – Canvas* developed from a tiny and rapid sketch made in a Natural History museum. The crusty three-dimensional character of this unusual shell suggested canvaswork, using alternations of raised stitches with much flatter and smoother ones. The choice of colour-scheme was arbitrary for this white shell, as the design had become fairly abstract, but the blues, fawns and greens related to the colours of the sea. The mainly woollen threads were contrasted with perlés and a few beads added to enhance the textural quality of the work.

For *Sea Urchin – Padded* (a piece of trapunto quilting) an increase in scale was needed. The design was built up in fabrics of varied textures of white and cream (some including a fine gold thread) plus pieces of gold kid and white plastic raised with felt. The fabric units were cut out, joined together and applied to a background of maple crash backed with firm cotton sheeting. Shapes were outlined with a wide satin stitch on the sewing-machine in preparation for padding. It was then mounted permanently on its wooden frame and the areas tightly padded through tiny slits cut in the back, then stitched up neatly. Of course, the larger the area padded, the fatter it becomes. A day was spent decorating the panel with gold threads, stitchery and beads, but these were subsequently removed as the sculptural quality and effects of light and shade were being lost; I found myself working from complexity towards simplicity.

When your various decisions have been made, you come next to the technical process of enlarging, etc, in preparation for the final stage of designing and making. Having a design 'blown up' on a photocopying machine can save time and ensures that the subtleties of the original drawing are accurately maintained.

***Garden Furniture** Sketches for a patchwork quilt design by Jean Colgan*

In developing the design in this way, deciding on methods, scale and so on, it is clear that some commitments regarding the kind of materials will have been made, though particular choices regarding individual fabrics, colours, textures and threads will not be made until the next and final stage of designing and making is reached (Chapter 4).

Beach Huts Sketches for a
design by Jean Colgan

Design for English quilting, to
form part of a larger design for
a coverlet, taken from a life
drawing by Jean Colgan

Sea Urchin – Canvaswork
18 x 20in (46 x 51cm)

Sea urchin sketch – rapidly
executed in a museum

Sea Urchin – Padded
25¹/₂ x 30¹/₂in (65 x 77cm),
using the same design as the
canvas work sea urchin

USING YOUR LETTERING

Having mastered cutting letter shapes, you might wish to design a panel in which lettering will be the main feature, or be used as a border, in both instances the letters comprising words. They might also be used individually to make a rag book or an alphabet panel as a group project, B for Beetle, T for Train, etc.

Another way would be to use the letters just for the pattern quality of their shapes and make them flow across the design like starlings in autumn or an army on the march, or to take a letter and use it, perhaps in mirror image, to make a border pattern for a garment.

For variety, take quite a different approach to designing from that described in the preceding section.

First, you will need some idea of the scale to which you will be working, in order to be able to estimate roughly the size of letters required. The letters can vary in size and in thickness, ie, a letter 6in (15cm) high could be ½in or 1½in (1.5 or 4cm), etc, in thickness of stroke, according to the effect you wish to achieve. Your largest letters could be the heaviest looking, but not necessarily so.

It is a good idea to choose several different sheets of paper, varying in tone from white through light, medium and dark greys to black, which could be achieved with newspapers, or you could work in colour, selecting areas from magazines and newspaper colour supplements, but still taking note of the contrasts in tone value. By folding and cutting through several layers of paper at the same time, produce quite a number of each of the letters you need, varying their size,

thickness and depth of tone. Prepare a background of plain, white, grey or coloured paper cut to the required measurements, or you could use fabric folded to size.

Now, begin to move your letters about on the background trying out your different letter variations, adding pieces of paper or fabric behind the letters to maintain dark on light, or the opposite, or trying different colours together. You will be playing with size, thickness and weight, depth of tone and possibly colour: quite a lot of aspects to consider! Take care that the space between the letters is not too great, or they will lose their impact and get 'lost' in a sea of background. Consider too, how they relate to the outside shape of your design. When the arrangement feels right, pin the letter shapes in place and fasten the design on the wall, then stand back and check that the placing is good, moving or replacing some of the pieces where necessary.

Kitty Weedon has translated her cut paper design into fabric in her panel *Cloudy* (overleaf), using overlaid nets which produce their own textural patterns, a thicker fabric and some running stitches in silver threads.

Another way would be to push your letters around on a background and, when you are happy with the placing, draw the background shape to suit them; this might be a better approach if you are using the letters in a free design.

In designing a border or pocket, etc, for a garment, you would need to start with the dress pattern shapes and decide on the sizes of the units, ensuring that the scale is appropriate and also how the repeat of the design would work at the seams.

You will now have a design prepared and the next stage is

to decide how best to carry it out. Perhaps you will quilt it as a bedcover, or cut out the letters in fabrics – leather, gold kid, etc, and apply them on a background varying in colour to complement the letter forms. Some of the letters could be carried out entirely in stitchery, their positions being tacked out using your paper patterns. Working in felt would offer interesting possibilities in layering, building up some letters and cutting others out from the surface to reveal another colour beneath.

Having decided on your method from the many available, you would make preparation in the usual way.

If you have enjoyed working with letters in this way, you might go on to study other letter forms by looking at the variety used in magazine advertisements, or studying books on lettering. Try inventing your own variations of letter forms, perhaps using thick and thin strokes instead of the block letters we have used so far. Greek and Russian alphabets also offer new ranges of possibilities!

On page 116 you can see a stole made by Pat Russell, who trained initially as a calligrapher. The lettering reads TAKE MY YOKE UPON YOU AND LEARN OF ME. In designing this piece of work Pat started with cut-paper letters in strips, so that each shape could be built up with great accuracy. Then the colour was organised to achieve a balance, sometimes the letter being lighter and sometimes darker than the background. The colours relate to each other on either side of the stole and a Y is cleverly placed in the centre of the curve at the back of the neck. The rich and varied fabrics are sewn down by machine and enriched with machine embroidery, braids, yarns and some embroidery threads, all worked on the machine.

DESIGNING FROM MARK-MAKING

As we have seen, your mark-making is likely to have produced a design that is fairly complete in itself, so the question now is which method will offer the best scope for exploiting those aspects of the design that caused you to choose it in the first place? Weigh up the pros and cons of the different methods that could be used and decide which attracts you most. Select a size appropriate to the method, enlarge the design if necessary and begin collecting your materials.

Designs using cut letters by
Anne Boutle

Stole by Pat Russell. The lettering reads: TAKE MY YOKE UPON YOU AND LEARN OF ME. It was designed using cut-paper strips and carried out in rich and varied fabrics with machine embroidery. *98in (2.48m) long*

Cloudy by Kitty Weedon. A panel resulting from experiments with folded and freely cut lettering. The back-up work is also interesting. *18 x 14in (46 x 35cm)*

DEVELOPING YOUR SAMPLES OF MANIPULATED FABRICS

Collect together the samples resulting from the various exercises you have undertaken and lay them out on a table. Examine them carefully to see which areas offer further development; no doubt you already know which you enjoyed most.

Below are some suggestions of ways in which you could explore your ideas further.

a   Increase the scale.

b   Repeat units several times over, perhaps varying them in some way.

c   Try combining two or more units.

d   Use one of the units as a central feature and design additional and complementary pieces.

e   Could you use any of your pieces in a different context?

f   If you have become enthusiastic about weaving, you might join a class, buy a loom, or produce a tapestry on a larger scale.

To what use could the results of this work be put? A wall-hanging? Dress embroidery? A useful object such as a bag, a cushion, a table-mat, etc?

DESIGNING FROM GEOMETRIC FORM

You may have produced sketches or photographs of aspects of geometric form found in the environment and these could be translated as already described.

If, for example, you have made drawings of Gothic or Saracenic architecture, artifacts, etc, try folding paper and cutting some of the arch shapes or other characteristic features. Try cutting a border pattern in paper and also a central square to make a cushion or a bag etc. Stick them on to a contrasting background, draw additional lines on both shapes and background (using a ruler, or compass) and consider how you could use this design in embroidery.

Cut out twenty-five crosses in paper and move them about to make patterns, then stick them down and do some additional drawing. Try working with other cut-out geometric units in the same way, perhaps varying the size, or combining, say, squares and circles. Diamonds could be interesting too. How about designing a pulpit fall in this way, using applied gold or silver kid with laid metal thread, or devising a design by layering felt?

How can you make use of what you have learned in your experiments with canvaswork stitches? A design based on

Pulpit Fall – 'cut out twenty-five crosses'. *14¹/₂ x 15¹/₂in (37 x 40cm)*

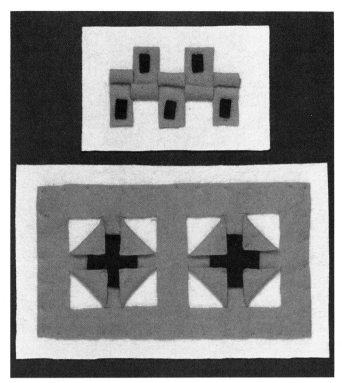

natural form might give you scope to develop further in this direction.

Ways of using strip patchwork may well have become obvious as you experimented with cutting and stitching the strips together. Have you thought of increasing the scale quite considerably and perhaps embarking on a quilt?

Designing using a geometry kit is likely to have resulted in some completed designs, requiring only to be scaled up to size.

The panel, *Vibrations* (overleaf) began by using a compass. The inspiration came from the paintings of Sonia Delaunay, who has made many explorations of colour based on circular forms. The design is built up mainly in rich transparent fabrics, with machine embroidery.

Julia Johnston's wall-hanging *Stars and Stripes* is another geometric piece. At some point she did a course on strip patchwork which she chose to carry out using patterned wrapping-paper assembled in strips and inserted between a layer of black tarlatan and a backing fabric to produce quite a small unit. Later, the idea was developed into this wall-hanging in which strips of black silk decorated with black sequins are stitched on top of the paper surfaces. Black needlecord is used to create a grid pattern. The design structure for the wall-hanging was first drawn out on paper and then developed in the materials themselves.

Cut-felt geometric units

Morning Stars by Donald Quantrill, using geometric form

119

Vibrations This was inspired by the painting of Sonia Delaunay and designed with a compass. It is built up using transparent fabrics and machine embroidery

STITCHERY AND METHODS

Throughout the history of embroidery, many stitches have been devised for use in various situations. Writers categorise them in different ways, sometimes according to their use, such as outline, open filling, solid filling, isolated stitches, etc, or how they are made, eg looped, chain, knotted, composite, etc, and those related to specific methods such as canvas, and drawn and pulled thread stitches, those suitable for embroidery on net, smocking and for edging, etc.

We have already looked at families of stitches and have perhaps worked the chain stitch sampler. Another versatile family is the buttonhole stitch which includes crossed, knotted, double, up and down, threaded, whipped, etc, plus a good selection of filling stitches, too (to quote from Barbara Snook's book *Embroidery Stitches*). Isabel Mulloy has used this stitch on her panel *Lava Moss* (see page 177).

Some people derive great pleasure from learning and using a rich variety of stitches and identifying them in historical examples. Others settle for a fairly limited number, achieving variety in their work by varying the colour, scale and texture of thread as suggested in Chapter 1 and looking for a new stitch to achieve some particular effect. Your own approach is a question of personal choice.

What seems most significant is the way in which stitches are used and whether they are expressing what is required of them. There is no great virtue in a display of virtuosity for its own sake: a City and Guild's student once used so many different stitches that her work was deemed 'vulgar' and she

Stars and Stripes by Julia Johnston. Strips of wrapping paper have been inserted between layers of black tarlatan and a backing fabric, black needlecord is used to form the grid pattern and the wall-hanging is decorated with black sequins. *41 x 67in (1.04 x 1.70m)*

Stitchery sampler by Charlotte Dew

apparently failed! This seems extreme, but perhaps it is a thought worth considering.

Some stitches are flat in character, while others have thickness or a knotted quality; sometimes it is useful to contrast these qualities in the same area. The choice of a square stitch might relate well to your particular design.

In building up an area of texture, great richness can be achieved by piling stitches on top of each other, as you will have discovered from the exercises that you have done. It is worth exploring the possible uses of any stitch that interests you, varying the size, the threads and how you use it, and also investigating other stitches in the same family.

It is interesting to note that different people using the same stitch will somehow produce different results and that stitching, like handwriting, can have a very personal quality.

Embroiderers differentiate between areas of work such as canvaswork and drawn threadwork by using the term *methods*. Traditional methods are established ways of working in which particular materials and procedures are used, leading to a recognisable result. For instance, hardanger embroidery from Norway is characterised by the 'Kloster' blocks, in which small rectangular groups of satin stitches are used to outline a cut space, across which some of the horizontal and vertical threads are left. These are worked with overcast or weaving stitches, then additional lace filling stitches are added. Further satin stitch blocks are arranged to enrich the spaces. The background fabrics used are linen or canvas, woven with double warp and weft so they are strong and do not fray in cutting. Incidentally, here is another method that is essentially geometric in design.

Embroiderers studying for City and Guilds examinations become familiar with a variety of such methods and learn something of their history. These may include appliqué, blackwork, canvaswork, counted threadwork, cutwork, drawn and pulled threadwork, goldwork, Mola art, needleweaving, net embroidery, pattern darning, patchwork, quilting, shadow work, and so on. All these methods have produced a rich heritage of embroidery.

The term *technique* is often avoided as it seems to imply a 'correct' way of doing things, thus offering the threat of rigid rules. To a certain extent a craft imposes its own discipline; if you do tent-stitch on a large piece of canvas without mounting it first it could become irretrievably distorted, so canvaswork demands being mounted on a stretcher. We need to recognise the difference between restrictions dictated by the craft itself and those imposed by a rigid mode of thinking. After all, every embroidery method has been invented by somebody; new ideas are constantly being devised and old ones updated and this brings great vitality to the craft. No method is sacrosanct and, so long as we respect the necessary limitations of the different procedures, their use should offer fluidity and freedom.

Embroidery methods are also affected by new tools that appear on the market.

Quiltmakers, for example, have evolved new and skilful ways of simplifying the technical aspects of their work and useful new tools to help them do so. The sewing-machine is a tool accepted everywhere, and indeed is often a highly sophisticated piece of equipment, but at one time a zigzagged edge had to be hidden or disguised! Some people focus entirely on this method with notable success. Alice Kettle has created a new and dramatic art form with machine embroidery, as in her work *Roundelay* (overleaf):

> This piece emerges from previous work. It can be viewed in isolation, but is part of a continuing development.
>
> A suggestion of the figure was drawn in thread, with the knowledge that this could change dramatically as I worked; the figure gives me a focus to identify with. Some background had to be established in order to give a context, but a substantial amount of the figure was done fairly early. The process is unplanned and depends upon mixing colour and upon the movement of the material. There are areas which I work and rework continually, if need be cutting out pieces which have become too thick, then inserting more material and sewing over and over; I discarded three faces before retaining the fourth.
>
> The size of a piece is dictated by what seems possible to complete in the available time when I begin. 'The larger the better' suits me. I use furnishing fabric and sew entirely by machine, choosing from a very great range of threads. It is both a demanding and an exciting experience.

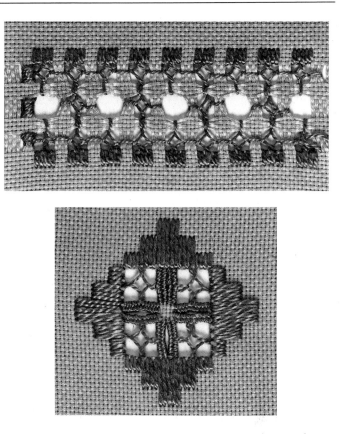

Hardanger samples on evenweave linen – small unit is *2in (5cm) square*

Hardanger using large-scale units on a coarse fabric by Isabel del Strother *10 x 7½in (25 x 19cm)*

This is not a book about specific methods and how to do them; there are many books available today which offer both suggestions for design approaches and technical information on many different methods (see Bibliography). However, a few interesting possibilities are described below.

MACHINE EMBROIDERY

The sewing-machine can be used as a means of holding fabrics neatly in place without having to turn under the edges. This is a great advance on the days when fabrics were stitched down laboriously with a buttonhole or herringbone stitch, which was necessary until the zigzag was added to the capabilities of ordinary sewing-machines. The zigzag used in this way can vary in size and either be open or a close satin stitch.

It is, of course, possible just to run a straight stitch near the edge of a piece of fabric as a means of attaching it, ignoring the raw edges.

Lines

Lines of straight-stitch machining can be worked with the sewing foot in place in the usual way and several rows of lines 'drawn' freely in this fashion can enrich a design.

Lines can also be worked using a satin stitch or close zigzag, which can be varied in width by adjusting the knob to and fro as you work.

A heavier line can be achieved by running, say, three woollen threads under a wide zigzag, then pausing to cut short first one and then another, gradually narrowing the width of the line until it tapers away to nothing.

Free machining using the darning foot

It is possible to make a tracery of fine lines using the darning foot, or removing the foot altogether and lowering the drop feed control or 'teeth'. It is usually necessary to mount your fabric in the base of a ring-frame so it lies flat on the bed of the machine. It needs to be as tight as a drum. Lay it on the machine and draw up the bottom thread through the fabric. After a few stitches these ends can be cut away. Now press your foot down fairly hard so the machine runs fast, while moving the frame slowly, with your fingers holding the fabric down just within the edge of the ring. You can move it forward or back, from side to side, or round in a circle; try exploring the different patterns you can make. It is also possible to use the zigzag in this way, as Aileen Murray has done in her panel *First Light*.

I worked this when exploring machine embroidery techniques and basing design on the Sussex landscape. I was chiefly interested in the quality of light and atmosphere in a small, deeply enclosed lane. The work started from a small sketch which was adapted and enlarged to a size related to the machine texture (it could not be too big). The main lines were marked on to a neutral linen union fabric with blueish dye. The shimmering quality of colour derives from the use of about twenty thread colours in greys and soft shades. It was worked on both domestic and Irish machines mainly using a zigzag

First Light by Aileen Murray. This panel was worked on both domestic and Irish sewing machines, using a zigzag stitch. About twenty thread colours in greys and soft shades were used to achieve the shimmering quality of colour. *15 x 20in (38 x 51cm)*

Roundelay by Alice Kettle. Machine embroidery. *22 x 29in (56 x 74cm)*

stitch. There are small areas of applied fabric and a very little hand stitching along the edge of the lane. It was a piece of work that went very easily, but required constant checking from a distance because of working so closely with a ring-frame. I kept building up across the whole piece: adding a further layer of colour and then reviewing progress.

Using a whip stitch

If you wish to build a denser texture on the surface and produce a whip stitch, tighten the top tension and, if necessary, loosen the bottom tension by very gradually releasing the tiny screw in the bobbin case until you get the result you require, but take care not to go too far and lose the screw! The result will be a looping of the base thread on the surface of the fabric.

Use of vanishing materials

Machine stitching can be worked on water soluble fabrics, but the stitches must create a mesh of some kind, so that when the base disappears, the pattern will still hold together. The fabric is removed by dissolving it in water – hot or cold depending on the type of fabric.

Working with metallic or uneven threads

You may wish to use a metallic thread, or one with a texture that could not be used through the needle without breaking or splitting. Such a thread can be wound on to the bobbin, by hand if necessary, and the machine stitching worked from the back of the fabric. A pencil line can be drawn as a guide, but you will not be able to see the effect until you have finished and can turn the work over, so it is advisable to do some preliminary experiments.

Holes and 'cobwebs'

A design can be developed on fine or heavy fabric in which the main feature is the cutting of holes which are embellished with cobweb-like machine embroidery. With the fabric held taut in a ring-frame, small circles or ovals can be outlined twice (to strengthen them), using the darning foot or removing it altogether. Next, cut away the fabric within the circle fairly close to the machine stitching and outline the holes carefully, using the zigzag on satin stitch with the zigzag foot in place.

It is now possible, using a free machine stitch with the foot off, to work across the circle and back again, so that the return stitches interlink with and strengthen the first ones. Travel round the circle, going over and back, and finally work round and round the centre to produce a cobweb-like result. Different coloured threads might be used on adjacent circles, perhaps varying quite subtly. Machine stitchery could be worked on the fabric between them and beads added – this offers possibilities for dress embroidery.

It is not always necessary to use a ring-frame in doing machine embroidery. If your fabric is very firm and stiff, or has become so through building up the work on the machine, then the frame may perhaps be discarded.

Rich and dense or open textures can be achieved with machine embroidery, either used on its own or combined with scraps of fabric, lace, beads, hand embroidery, etc.

Holes and Cobwebs

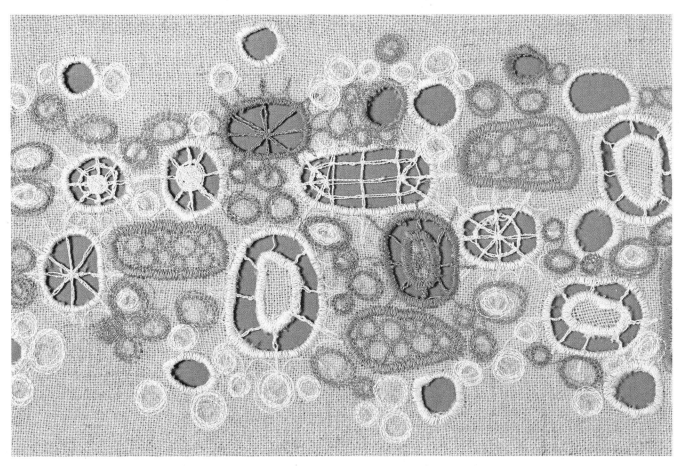

QUILTING, PATCHWORK AND PADDING

Quilting and padding present considerable scope for the embroiderer. Traditionally there are three types of quilting: English, Italian and trapunto, English quilting often being combined with patchwork (piecing). Stumpwork was popular in the seventeenth century; figures raised in high relief were included in the embroidery on cushions, book covers, caskets and cabinets, etc, some of the raised shapes being made of wood covered with fabrics and stitchery. All these methods have been used afresh in recent times and all offer a rich potential.

English quilting

In this method a padding material is sandwiched between the surface material, or 'top', and the backing. The stitching is done through these three layers, drawing the fabrics tightly together, allowing them to puff up between the lines of quilting. This method depends very much on the play of light on the subtly curving surfaces. The fabrics used can be matt, such as cottons, Viyella, etc, or shiny silks or satins. We have a heritage of many quilts and garments made in this way from the seventeenth century onwards.

Margaret Rivers' quilt, *The Longest Walk Taken by a Line* (overleaf), is based on a photograph of reflections in windows. These were drawn, simplified and abstracted, as can be seen on the design sheets, and finished up as a continuous line 'drawn' freely on a quilt with a sewing-machine.

It is worked in twenty-five blocks, each 12in (30cm) square, the top being Habutai silk. There is a layer of terylene wadding (batting) and a backing of heavy lawn. The machine thread used is of a random shading from white into grey, with a yellow silk on the bobbin. Each square was worked separately without a frame, using a darning foot with the feed dropped. When completed the squares were laid face to face

in turn, excess wadding (batting) cut away, then seamed together on the machine and the back fabric turned in and stitched by hand.

Alternatively, the 'top' is often patchwork (piecing) and then the quilting is worked in relation to the design, either 'in the ditch', which means along the joins, or in other ways to enhance the effect and to add light and shade in some particular way.

The padding material can be something fairly thin like domette, or layers of sheep's wool, a woolly blanket or synthetic polyester wadding (batting), which comes in different thicknesses, and the backing a plain or patterned supporting cotton or other fabric relating to the top.

The three layers must be assembled, smoothed and tacked together, working from the centre to the edges making sure that all lie together with even tension. Tack many lines in both directions. Quilting can be done by hand or on a sewing-machine. Many machines now have a 'walking foot' which helps avoid uneven pulling of the fabrics.

Patchwork

Patchwork is very popular today and good cotton fabrics are available, both plain and patterned, in a great range of colours. Many people also enjoy using up their dress-making off-cuts, which can be quite nostalgic! It is advisable to wash all the fabrics first to deal with problems of shrinkage and colour-running. There are many traditional designs, mainly geometric, with appealing names like 'Grandmother's Flower Garden' or 'Oak Leaf Quilt', etc, but it is more interesting to evolve one's own.

Some years ago I experimented with piecing free curves. *Lilies* (page 2) is one of a series worked in this way. The design expresses my delight at observing the unfurling of these handsome flowers. The first stage in the design was a tonal drawing in pencil emphasising the strong rhythmic

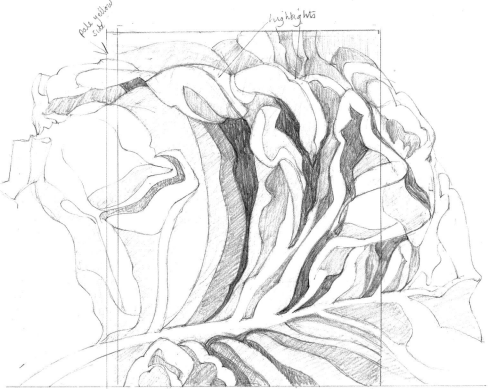

Lettuce Leaf Patchwork design

The Longest Walk Taken by a Line This is a detail of a wall-hanging by Margaret Rivers. The design is based on reflections in windows and is built up of twenty-five blocks, which were quilted on the sewing machine by 'drawing' freely with the needle. *54in (1.37m) square*

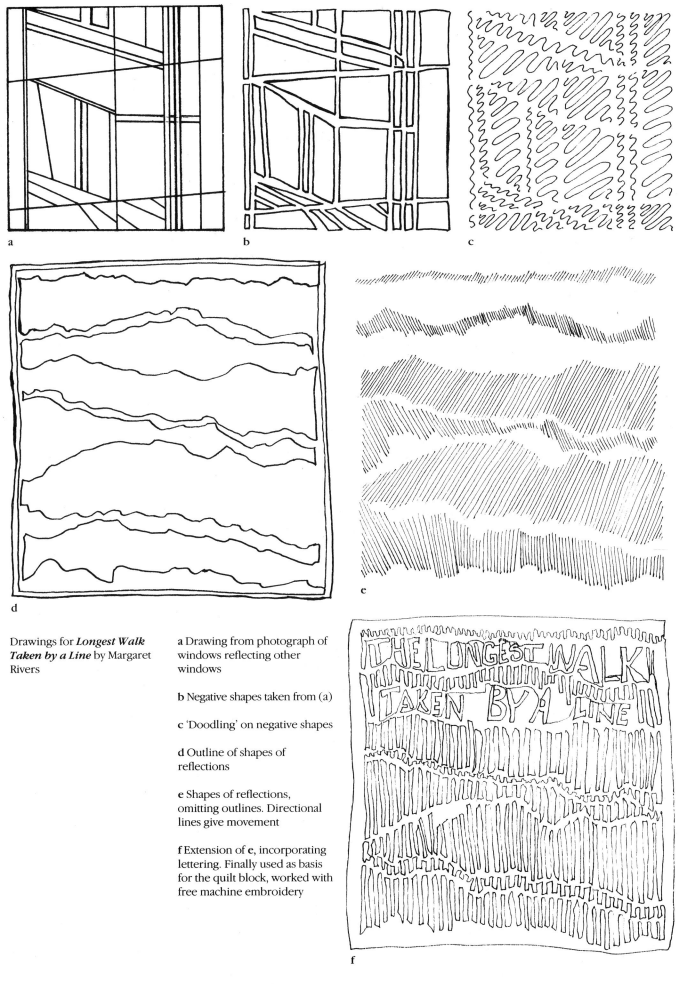

Drawings for *Longest Walk Taken by a Line* by Margaret Rivers

a Drawing from photograph of windows reflecting other windows

b Negative shapes taken from (a)

c 'Doodling' on negative shapes

d Outline of shapes of reflections

e Shapes of reflections, omitting outlines. Directional lines give movement

f Extension of **e**, incorporating lettering. Finally used as basis for the quilt block, worked with free machine embroidery

Drawing for *Lilies* Patchwork

(*opposite*)
Leaves and Lilies Patchwork
design

qualities, which was then enlarged by squaring up on cartridge paper. The enlarged design was traced through on to a
second sheet, so that there was one for pinning on the wall
and one to cut up into pattern pieces, each numbered and
marked with a vertical and horizontal line. I spent weeks
selecting the fabrics and, as so often, found myself simplifying, reducing the number of fabrics used, and keeping some
for stems only as the design became confused if they were
used for leaves as well.

Making up was a long slow task. All the pieces were cut out
carefully, true to the grain-line of the fabrics and with a small
turning allowed. These were then re-pinned on top of the
paper, the edges turned over firmly and tacked, avoiding any
pulling, and clipped where necessary. Two of these paper-
lined pieces would be placed to fit exactly, and pinned at

either end of a curve, then turned carefully face to face and
oversewn together by curving the pieces over my fingers,
moving them this way and that to make the edges match and
unpicking now and then. Eventually the papers were removed, the wall-hanging was backed and finished with
borders and a lining. See Chapter 7 for making up.

Italian quilting
This is worked with a surface fabric and a backing of butter-
muslin, or other soft cotton, which are tacked together. It is a
linear method and the finished effect is of a raised line on a
flat surface. Double lines are drawn on the back and are
either machined or hand stitched through both fabrics, then a
thick soft wool is threaded between them, using a large blunt
needle.

Traditionally the lines are even in width and continuous. Where they intersect the thread is pulled out at the back and reinserted, leaving a small loop to allow for shrinkage. Cottons, or richer looking silky fabrics were often used for cushion covers, bags, etc.

The method is capable of wider uses. The two lines need not stay of equal width and, as they widen, additional threads can be pushed through from the back to produce greater variety and refinement. Perhaps matt and shiny fabrics can be collaged together and then the lines of quilting will have a quality of contrast.

If white cotton organdie is laid over a white cotton backing and Italian quilting is worked in lines of varying widths, using fat woollen threads in strong bright colours, and perhaps mixing the colours and tones across the width of a line, some interesting effects can be achieved, as the organdie modifies the colours which become soft and muted.

Such approaches could be combined with other methods to achieve some particular desired effects, as in the panel *Rocks and Pines, Algarve* (overleaf). This is another landscape in my present series of rocks and pine trees, inspired by the beaches of the Algarve in southern Portugal, with the sandy cliffs, pine trees, caves and seaweed covered boulders. The work was designed in layers, with fine chiffon and nets for sky and trees, Italian quilting of cotton fabrics for the cliffs, lightly padded velvets and corduroys to bring the rocks forward and heavier trapunto quilting for the foreground. Flystitch was initially used in fine threads on the trees, but this was rejected in favour of long diagonal straight stitches.

Padding, trapunto quilting and soft sculpture

Trapunto quilting involves using two layers of fabric, one for the top, plus a firm cotton backing. Shapes are outlined with the sewing-machine and then a slit is made in the backing fabric and padding material (such as Kapok or polyester wadding) pushed into the shape a little at a time, using scissor points or a steel crochet hook. If too much padding is used it may distort the fabric, or cause it to pull away from the surface. When the area is padded to your liking, the slit is then neatly stitched up again.

If the shapes are small and only to be lightly padded, it may not be necessary to use a stretcher. If, however, you plan to make the sculptural quality the main feature, and to pad to capacity, it is important to mount the work on a wooden stretcher, preferably permanently, as the padding will distort the fabrics so much that to mount it later would be almost impossible. Padding will, of course, swell downwards as well as upwards, hence the need for a stretcher rather than board for the final mounting. Another feature to remember when designing your panel is that the larger the area to be padded, the higher it will rise from the surface.

When you have prepared your design, a plan of action needs to be made before you start on your project.

Any machine embroidery on the surfaces to be padded would have to be done before the backing is added. Hand embroidery could be done at this time also, or might be worked at a final stage on top of the padding.

If you intend to apply fabrics to the surface it is wise to join them together in a patchwork manner if possible and to turn under the edges and work round them with a satin stitch on the sewing-machine, to avoid their pulling away when the padding is inserted.

This method has much to offer. It can be used with a single fabric for the top, which could be calico, wool, silk or hessian, etc, the fabric relating to the scale of the work. Alternatively, the padding could be used along with a variety of colours and textures, either allowing the fabrics to 'speak for themselves', unadorned, or be richly encrusted with stitchery and beads.

If trapunto padding can be a type of low relief sculpture, there is only a small shift from that to soft sculpture and work 'in the round'. Claes Oldenburg, the American artist, pioneered soft sculpture in the 1960s and a number of people have followed suit.

Gillian Harvey, for example, was inspired by rock crystals. She spent long hours drawing at the London Geological Museum until she had a sketch-book full of excellent reference material. She then worked in calico, combining English quilting with additional trapunto padding, and made three-dimensional units which she applied on the quilted surface. The qualities of the crystals inspired the use of tucks and smocking techniques, which the chosen fabric – calico – suited. The finished panel, *Rock Crystals,* is illustrated overleaf.

Recently there has been an interesting development in creating padded figures, either free-standing or in high relief, with hands and faces modelled in padding material covered with nylon tights (panty hose). I first saw this done by Rozanne Hawksley in the mid 1970s. The figures are very expressive, sometimes witty and sometimes tragic (see her piece... *et ne nos inducas... (... and lead us not...*) and also a panel in soft sculpture by Clem Gilder (pages 40–1)).

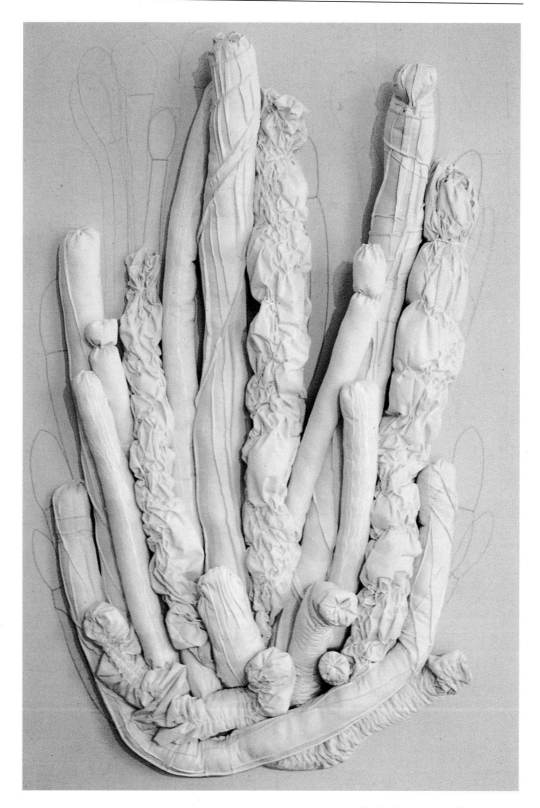

Rock Crystals by Gillian Harvey. This calico panel shows inventive use of quilting and padding, tucks and smocking techniques

Rock and Pines, Algarve The landscape is built up in layers. Italian quilting is used for the sandy cliffs and trapunto padding for the rocks in the foreground. *17 x 24in (43 x 61cm)*

133

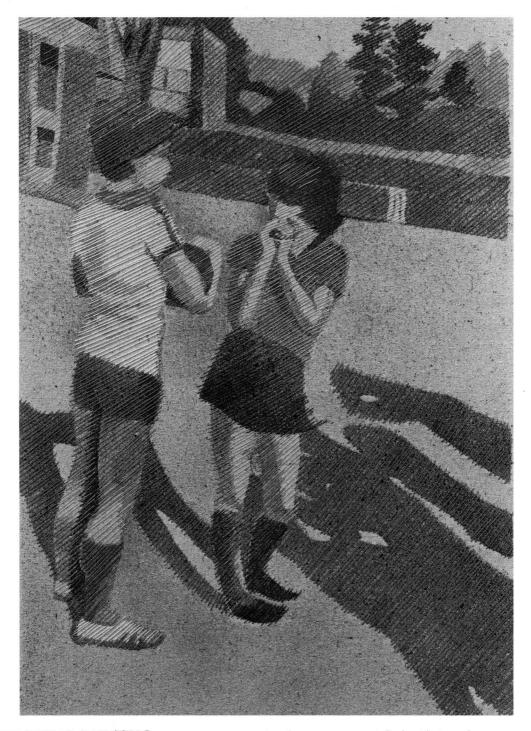

Boy and Girl, example of spray-painting using tooth-brush spatter and paper templates.
10 x 14in (25 x 36cm)

ADDING COLOUR BY DRAWING, PAINTING OR SPRAY-PAINTING

Many people these days add colour to their embroidery by using transfer crayons, or transfer paints. This involves drawing or painting on paper and transferring the image by placing it face-downwards on the fabric, covering the back with a sheet of paper and ironing it at the appropriate temperature. Usually synthetic fabrics have to be used.

There are also paints for silk and for cotton which can produce beautiful rich colour qualities. A gutta pen, which acts as a resist, can be used to outline certain areas and confine the dyes if you wish.

Valerie Quay has used fabric paints in her piece *Dusk*
This design was originally inspired by delphiniums glowing with colour at dusk. I began with a realistic interpretation but was not satisfied with it and so gradually the shapes and design evolved. The small squares (bottom left) represent the other smaller flowers surrounding the delphiniums. It is a mixture of pieced and applied work using bought colours although some of the greens and all the background colours were painted with fabric paints on to cotton lawn. The border is in two shades of mauve with some of the diagonal quilting lines continued right out to the edges.

Spray-painting
Spray-painting offers another means of adding colour to a fabric. It is a 'messy' method, so you will need to wear old clothes and to protect the floor, tables, walls.

Toothbrush spatter presents a very simple way of working,

Drawing for spray-painting templates

but one that works well on a small scale. The spatter marks vary in size and regularity and thus avoid a mechanical look. You will need a toothbrush and a small knife, some fabric-printing inks or dyes with a 'binder', or thickener. Mix three tones of black or a colour, light, medium and dark, in egg cups or small jars and have a paintbrush for each.

The technique is to brush the dye across the toothbrush, work it for a moment on paper to spread it evenly and then stroke the bristles towards yourself with the knife, which will produce the spray on a piece of scrap paper. You will soon master this simple technique.

Now iron a piece of calico or other fabric oddment, pin it out on a drawing-board and lay it on a table. Try cutting one or two paper templates out of newsprint, fastening them down with double-sided tape and spraying them, aiming to create a dark tone round one, grading away softly, and a lighter tone round the other. When you lift the paper you will observe the hard edge that has been created. Try moving the templates and see what happens. Then mix a few colours and explore these in a similar fashion until you feel quite at ease with the technique. Templates can be both negative or positive, ie, either the shape or the hole it was cut out of.

A commercial car-spray achieves a similar effect, and works well on quite a large scale. Again mix small amounts of fabric inks or dyes with a binder and dilute with a little water. 'Dab out' some of the colour on paper to test the colour and strength. When this is satisfactory, pour it into the spray jar through a piece of nylon tights (panty hose) fabric to get rid of any lumps. Screw the jar in place according to the instructions and try out the spray on paper pinned to a drawing-board and leaning against a wall. If the dye runs down, it needs to be thickened. When satisfied, work on your fabric.

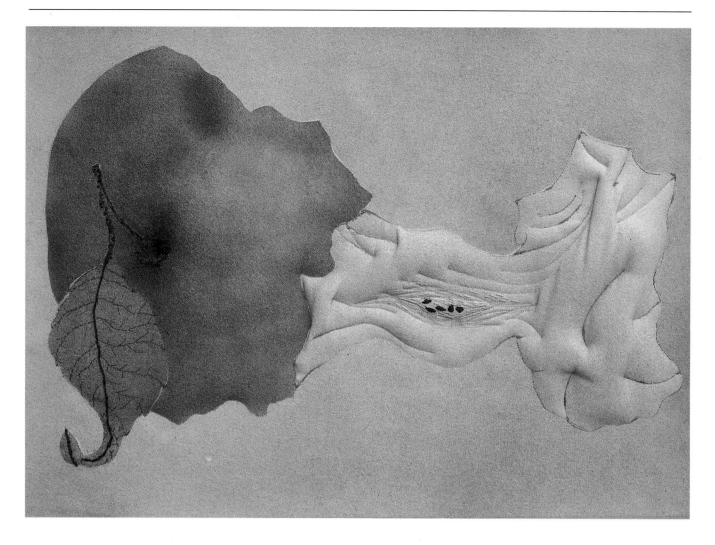

Apple Core by Helen Constable. The design was spray painted using cut stencils, then machined on to a backing fabric and mounted on a wooden frame. Finally it was padded heavily from the back. *29 x 21in (74 x 53cm)*

Helen Constable has used this method on her panel *Apple Core*. This piece of work came about through the study of fruit in a variety of two-dimensional media, culminating in this representation in bas-relief.

I started by cutting four stencils out of fairly substantial card – one the shape of the inner core, one for the outer apple skin, one for the leaf and a negative stencil to cover both these areas and leave the background exposed.

I then sprayed through the first two stencils in turn to produce the core and the outer skin, leaving a small area without the red to highlight the shiny surface of the fruit.

The leaf was produced in the same way, then the entire fruit was covered with the remaining stencil and the background was sprayed. The whole piece was sewn on to a backing cloth, following the outline of the apple, each part was then padded from the back of the work, in trapunto style. Finally the details were embroidered on, using silk threads.

There are other refined sprays available but they are not cheap. If this method appeals to you, you may decide to invest in such equipment.

A stencil brush is another possibility, to be used with the same inks or dyes; it produces a slightly coarser effect than the sprays.

Fabric dyes combined with the appropriate binder will have permanence if the fabrics are afterwards ironed on the back for quite a while at the appropriate temperature.

Dusk by Valerie Quay. The design was inspired by delphiniums at dusk. It is a mixture of pieced and applied fabrics, some of them coloured with fabric paints, and it is quilted. *22¹/₂ x 23in (57 x 58cm)*

COMBINING EMBROIDERY WITH OTHER MEDIA

It is sometimes challenging to extend the boundaries of embroidery by combining it with other media. Here are some suggestions for using embroidery along with different types of print-making, with tie-dye and with pottery.

Printing and embroidery
There are different ways of combining printing and embroidery using methods such as potato printing, block printing, screen printing and etching.

Potato printing
Potato printing offers a simple introduction to print-making, because the materials required are easily at hand, it is effective and it can also be done by children.

Materials required
> A few potatoes
> A knife
> Lino-cutting tools (optional)
> Poster paint and a large cheap water-colour brush
> Plenty of cheap paper (for printing on)
> Newspapers (to protect the table)

Method
Make a clean cut through the potato to give a very flat surface. Retain the shape of the potato and cut away a simple design using the knife or lino-cutting tools. Now paint the top surface of the block with fairly thick paint in a strong colour, or black, and press it firmly face-downwards on the paper. When you have found the right consistency for your paint print a pattern with your block, either a formal repeat or a free design, but placing the units close together.

Keep experimenting, perhaps cutting one or two additional blocks and trying out all sorts of arrangements with them; but do try to resist constantly discarding and cutting fresh blocks. Alternatively blocks can be cut in square or rectangular shapes, etc, and printed to touch each other in an all-over pattern.

These blocks could be printed on fabric; the paint would not be permanent though this might not matter with young children. Oil-bound printing ink cannot be used as the water in the potato would act as a resist. There is, however, a means of making permanent potato prints on cotton.

Boil pieces of white all-cotton fabric in a dye-bath of, say, one teaspoonful of potassium permanganate to a litre of water, adjusting the quantities to suit your requirements. This chemical can be obtained cheaply from a chemist (druggist) and, though purplish in colour, will dye the fabric a gingery brown. Press the fabric and print a design on it with a potato block painted with lemon juice. The colour will be discharged like magic, leaving a white print on a brown background. Diluted lemon juice can give a paler tone of golden brown.

As with the first method, the design can be formal or free and can offer an interesting starting point for an embroidery.

The design for Margaret Pascoe's lampshade (overleaf) resulted from printing in this way, the shapes relating to the natural markings on the Cornish Serpentine stone stand. Prints were made freely from two half potatoes of different sizes on a piece of sheeting, the design was then traced off and transferred to a piece of white organdie. Several experimental pieces were made, filling in the shapes with free machine embroidery, and the most pleasing was selected. Sometimes the background of the circular shape was filled and sometimes the centre pattern, to give positive and negative shapes. Hand stitching was added, using perlés and crochet cotton in white and cream. After stitching, some small holes were carefully cut in the organdie to let more light through the shade.

The embroidery was mounted on a purchased frame, a lining sewn in, and the top and bottom edges covered with white velvet ribbon.

Lino-block printing
Fabrics were traditionally printed with blocks of wood or metal and, as with a potato block, when the top surface was covered with printing ink and pressed face-downwards on fabric, would produce a print.

The design is initially drawn on the block and the unwanted areas cut away with knives and gouges of different sizes. Printing from the top surface this way is known as 'relief printing'.

Block-printing can become a more accessible method if linoleum is used instead of wood. It needs to have a smooth untextured surface and the old-fashioned brown kind is best. It cuts more successfully if warmed, perhaps against a radiator, when it becomes more pliable. Some of the synthetic materials used for floor tiles may work; one must experiment.

Lino tools are either various types of gouges, or special nibs which can be set into wooden handles. These vary in shape, such as 'u' and 'v' cutters, which come in different sizes, and there are also sharp blades for outlining. These tools produce different types of marks so explore this aspect on a spare bit of lino and take a print from it, to discover the potential of the medium.

Now draw an outline design on the block using a biro (ballpoint) pen, which will not wash off with water or turpentine when you clean up the block after taking trial prints or 'proofs' during the cutting, to check your progress. Cut freely within the guide lines of the drawing, exploiting the textural possibilities, and perhaps contrasting fine patterns with a broader style of cutting.

Blocks can be surfaced with flocking power to increase absorbency of ink, which is useful, though not essential when printing on fabric.

Blocks must be 'inked up' for printing, which means, firstly, mixing lino-printing inks with a small palette knife near the farther edge of a sheet of glass or smooth plastic, until the right colour is obtained. Next, spread some of this on a lino-roller and 'knock it out' in the middle of the piece of glass, sometimes lifting the roller to present a fresh surface to the ink, and rolling it in different directions until a smooth, even layer has been produced. Now roll it across the block, changing direction and making sure the corners and edges are well inked.

To print, place the block face-downwards in position on the fabric, which has been stretched and pinned out evenly on a flat board, cover the back with a piece of thin paper such as newsprint and roll across it quite heavily with a clean roller, taking care not to let it move.

A small block can be used for an all-over repeating pattern or a free design and later, when dry, enriched with stitchery. If the block is a large one it needs to be mounted on a piece of

Lino print by Kitty Weedon for *Butterfly* (overleaf)

plywood; 'marine' quality is ideal. A print is made by striking the block once in each corner and once in the centre, with the handle of a heavy mallet held upright. Alternatively it can be printed on an Albion type press, perhaps available at a local adult education centre.

Kitty Weedon designed a symmetrical butterfly on a lino block, cut it and printed it on two pieces of fabric which she stiffened with iron-on Vilene (fusible webbing) and laid together to give the back and the underside of the butterfly. These were then overlaid with different coloured nets. She worked round the edges with a zigzag on the sewing-machine, adding a fine florists' wire to stiffen it further. The antennae and legs were of wire threaded through tiny beads. It stands on a leaf of white silk with dacron padding and net overlay at the edges; a broken pearl necklace is used to make the pistil.

Monoprint
Printing-ink can be spread on a sheet of glass by one of the mark-making methods to create a pattern of marks and textures or a more considered image. Lay a sheet of paper on top and take a print using a small hand-roller. It is called a monoprint because normally you can only take one proof from it, though sometimes a second one may be obtained.

Christmas card lino print by Stan Dobbin

Butterfly by Kitty Weedon. A lino-block is printed on stiffened fabrics overlaid with coloured nets. Wire is threaded through tiny beads for the antennae and legs and the butterfly stands on a padded leaf. *8 x 9in (20 x 23cm)*

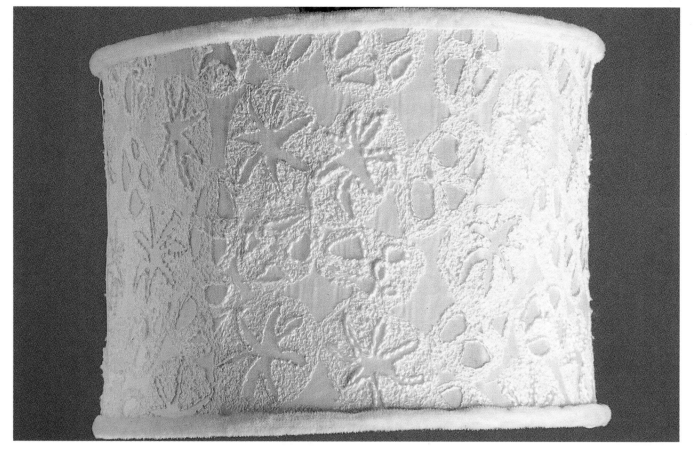

Experiment with different designs and with using just one colour or several. Now take some prints on pieces of fabric. Later you could work into your print with stitches, or design carefully on the glass for a particular piece of work.

Vicky Lugg has used a monoprint in gold fabric-paint in her panel *Circles and Squares*. This is one of a series of pieces inspired by the colour and patterns of Indian textiles. It is worked on a hand-dyed coarsely woven background with applied fabrics, hand stitching in gold and silk threads with added spangles and hand-made beads. See also Susan Wells' monoprint on page 146.

Screen-printing

Nowadays screen-printing is a commonly used method of printing dress and furnishing fabrics and also a respected method of print-making on paper.

A screen consists of a strong wooden frame across which is

Circles and Squares by Vicky Lugg. The embroiderer was inspired by the colour and patterns of Indian textiles and used a mono-print in gold fabric paint. *8in (20cm) square*

Lampshade by Margaret Pascoe. The design came from potato prints, which were traced and transferred to white organdie, embroidered by machine and hand stitched using perlé threads

Screen print design in three overlapping transparent colours

stretched some cotton or terylene organdie, and it must lie quite flat on the table, fabric side down, without any unevenness or twist. The inside of the frame and margins round the outside edges of the organdie are protected by gum-strip which has first been damped, then carefully positioned.

Screen-printing is essentially a stencil method, so the areas where colour is not required must be protected by one of several means. The simplest is to cut or tear newsprint, which will adhere to the underside of the screen when the first print is taken. Alternatives are to use special screen stencil material such as 'amber', or to paint out the background areas using varnish, or to use photographic means. A print is made using a fairly liquid ink which is pressed through the screen on to a paper or fabric beneath it, using a squeegee (a strip of rubber held in a wooden handle), which is slightly shorter than the inside width of the screen.

Designs can be built up in one colour or in several, in a spontaneous way or carefully planned so that colours 'register' (fit together) exactly. Either way, the changes of colours as they overlap each other can be exploited.

Screen-printed designs on fabric offer considerable scope to the embroiderer. They can be padded or enriched with stitchery, knitting, beads, sequins, ribbons, etc.

Screen-printing is often taught in secondary schools and is on offer at many adult education centres.

Etching
An etching is produced by covering a copper or aluminium plate with a brown-coloured acid-resist, then drawing with a variety of tools, conventional or otherwise, to remove the resist from the metal surface. The edges and back of the plate are then covered with a protective varnish and the plate submerged in acid which bites into the exposed metal. After this, the plate is cleaned, inked up and printed.

The lightest tone in the previous design is printed as a border pattern with applied diamond shapes in fabric and machine embroidery

The same screen used differently with machine embroidery for a child's dress

Etching on paper for *The Queen and the Beefeaters*

In this method the ink is pressed into the lines of the warmed printing plate, so printing is not from the top surface, as in relief printing, but from the varying depths of the lines. This is known as 'intaglio' printing.

Many years ago I saw a picture of the Queen and the Beefeaters in a newspaper colour supplement and found it rather amusing. I made a large drawing from it, and someone suggested developing the idea as an etching. This was successful, printing clearly on paper, velvet, chamois leather and various fabrics. Felt was the only fabric where the precision of line was lost. The pieces of printed fabrics were used to make a collage, with chamois leather for faces and the addition of a few cords and a sequin.

In combining etching with embroidery, the intention should be envisaged from the start and the etching specially designed to ensure that the embroidery will harmonise with the particular qualities of the etched line.

Etching is obviously a very specialised area requiring its

The Queen and the Beefeaters
An etching printed on fabrics and chamois leather, which were assembled into a collage. *22¹/₂ x 27¹/₂in (57 x 70cm)*

Monoprint by Susan Wells

Leaves are ideal sources for
design ideas

Tie-dye sample by Anne Maile,
using stitched lines

own materials, equipment and an etching press, but many
adult education establishments offer this type of facility, as do
some secondary schools.

Tie-dye

Tie-dye is a simple method requiring minimal equipment
and is therefore very suitable for using at home or in schools.
In the hands of a skilled craftsperson or artist, however,
highly sophisticated results can be produced.

Method

Lay a small piece of white cotton fabric flat on the table and
place a pebble in the middle of it. Draw up the fabric round
the pebble, first holding the corners, then hold the pebble
and pull the fabric together fairly evenly. Now bind it very
tightly close to the pebble, using a piece of string wound
round several times then knotted; more string could be tied
further away. Now boil the fabric in a dye-bath, or use cold
water dyes.

When dry, undo the string, which will have protected the
fabric to a certain extent from the dye, but allowed fine lines
of dye to creep through, so there will be a coloured area
round the pebble and irregular rings around this.

Other ways of exploring tie-dye are to run stitches in lines,
circles, etc, in the fabric and then draw up the thread, or
threads, very tightly before dyeing. Fabric can also be pleated
and wrapped tightly with string or rubber bands – the patterns produced could not be achieved by other means. They
could be developed further with machine embroidery or
hand stitching, etc, as in the large wall-panel illustrated.

Pottery

An example of an unusual and interesting combination of
pottery with trapunto quilting and stitchery is the work done
by Gail Burton. She made a number of pottery units, each
pierced several times near the base, so they could be stitched
into position. She then placed them in various arrangements
on a larger sheet of paper until she was satisfied with the
result. She drew round every piece, numbering it and record-

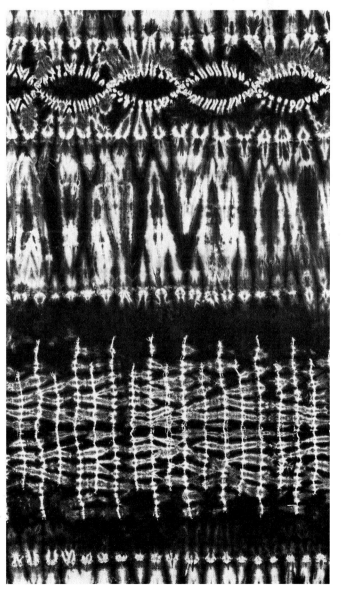

147

Hanging Garden, a project carried out by children aged nine to eleven, using tie-dye, Suffolk puffs and hand stitchery. Teacher – Judy Faulkner

Orchids by Gail Burton. An unusual combination of pinched earthenware clay, biscuit-fired only, and trapunto padded fabric. *17 x 22in (43 x 56cm)*

ing its position. Next, and working on the same sheet of paper, she sketched out various possibilities for incorporating the groups of pottery into related padded areas and made her final decisions.

Maple crash was used for the backgrounds, which padded nicely and harmonised well with the pottery. A series of quite large panels resulted, some of them also incorporating hand stitchery. *Orchids* is one of these pieces:

> The initial idea was to bring together two media which would normally be considered incompatible, to 'marry' them in such a way that they would complement and support each other.
>
> The subject of the work was inspired by floral forms. The media chosen were fabric and clay and each required a delicate and subtle approach to reflect the character of the subject.

Firstly, the clay forms were gently pinched and shaped from an earthenware clay and biscuit-fired only, in order to retain natural quality and colour. They were then placed on to a finely textured pale fabric which had been designed and padded to enhance the shapes and add depth and movement.

Finally, stamens were added. These were shaped from wire and bound with shades of mauve and pink thread to provide a subtle colour contrast and balance to the work as a whole.

In considering the combination of embroidery with another medium, it is important to recognise the characteristics of each and to feel that they really could enhance each other. A richly textured medium such as batik, for example, might not be suitable in that it would probably be distracting and confusing to combine it with embroidery.

CHAPTER 4

MAKING AND PROBLEM SOLVING

Here you are then, all ready to embark on the actual embroidery. The design has emerged through the work you have done in the previous stages and, as you have been making your own choices all along the line checking that you are following your original intentions, or discarding them for a good reason, you are now set to produce something that has a real personal quality.

How can the essence of your ideas and feelings, worked out in design form, be held on to and strengthened as the work develops? Perhaps you have captured these aspects by emphasising certain qualities of shape, the rhythm of lines, tone and texture, etc. These are undoubtedly very important in giving strength of form to the work and need to be kept constantly in mind. Remember, however, that the symbolic meanings are also highly significant; the pattern of the waves on the sea may express a feeling of serenity and peace, or of threat, though such meanings may not necessarily come through at the conscious level.

Whether you are enchanted at seeing the sun glistening on wet cobwebs amongst the raspberry bushes or are specially interested in the subtle variations of colour and tone you have seen in the set of white china on a white tea-tray, your idea and feeling is at the heart of the matter and you must keep hold of this. Susan Free's description of the inspiration for *Dark Sea* (overleaf) bears this out.

I found the muslin folded in the art cupboard and had never seen so much before. I wanted to touch it and began pulling and ruffling with the bulk of the fabric still in the cupboard. I played like a child would, tossing it and letting it fall, fluffing it up and trapping the air momentarily to see it sink into soft forms. It was mesmerising. As it was now in a mess I took it to a large work-top to continue my games.

I was reminded of the end of a wave when the foam rushes to the shore and dissolves on the wet sand and set to work to fix the image. I had to work very quickly before the feeling was lost.

The strong narrow shape took over and, to trap the air, I decided to quilt and pad. But the muslin took on a much heavier and harder form which had

Who does she think she is?
Fancies herself: finished design
by Jean Colgan

150

not been there in my initial playing. Its bolder appearance needed colour to depict the darker side of the sea at night. The only tool available to give instant colour was a tin of car-spray. Then the whole thing was trapped in a dark wooden frame.

It has been claimed that 'inspiration never delivers a finished work' and that, usually, we are not able to foresee the finished result in our mind's eye. How boring that would be anyway, as we should lose so much of the sense of adventure, of needing to consider the various options and then make a choice at every stage throughout the work.

As you begin translating your design into fabrics and threads, the nature and possibilities of the materials and the particular characteristics of the method chosen will together influence the style of the finished piece of work. As previously stated, a method will impose its own discipline and limitations on the work to some extent, as well as offering special qualities to be explored and developed in a way that you will choose.

Now is the time for collecting together all the suitable materials you can possibly find. Arrange them in groups, selecting and rejecting until your decisions are made. As you do this you will become aware of their different qualities and of subtle relationships in colour and tone. Unusual combinations may present themselves, giving a special thrill of delight, or suggesting the use of unexpected opposites here and there, like hints of reds to enliven the greens in a predominantly green colour scheme. Even if you are working in white on white, you will realise how threads differ in thickness, texture and whiteness. You may feel you can mix wools, cottons, silks, etc, or know at once that you must restrict yourself to cotton only.

It is necessary to have a general idea of procedure, so that you can carry out your intentions in a sequence that works in practice. Machining will have to be done before the fabrics are mounted on a larger frame and spray painting will probably need to be completed at an early stage, unless you plan to spray your stitchery! It is usually a good idea to work all over a piece of embroidery, building it up gradually and in a general way, rather than to complete a particular area and risk finding it out of context as the work develops. Focussing on the essential qualities of the design should help you decide whether the textural enrichment that stitchery offers is adding intensity to the image, or whether you are being carried away by the pleasure of stitching and losing sight of the relation of this part to the whole.

People often ask how neat the back of the work should be. The answer is a practical one: it should be neat where the wrong side will be seen and strong enough to do its job. A garment, cushion cover, table-mat, etc, must be capable of being washed or cleaned many times without looking unsightly or coming undone, so needs careful finishing. A panel or wall-hanging however, need not be as neat on the back, with all the machining ends tied up etc, as they will not be seen or submitted to heavy use, but it is important that hand stitching is firmly fastened off. Knots can be used so long as they are strong and will not come undone.

Remember to put your work up on the wall periodically and stand back to assess your progress and judge how best to proceed. It is disappointing to realise that a section you en-

Design by Sarah Hosking

Cat by Susan Wells

151

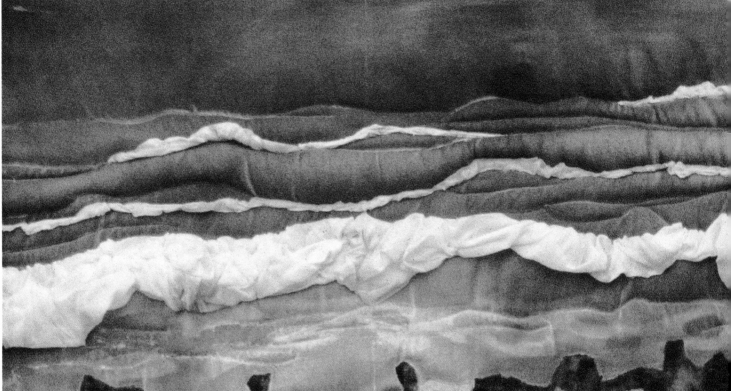

Still, Quite Still by Shân Taylor. This piece is worked on finely woven silk canvas using dyes and one simple linear stitch, and 'attempts to compress time into a frozen moment'

Dark Sea by Susan Free. 'I played like a child with the muslin and was reminded of a wave when the foam rushes to the shore'. It is padded and coloured with car-spray. *45¹/₂ x 18in (116 x 46cm)*

153

joyed doing is not very satisfactory and needs to be unpicked, but this is part of the process and happens to us all from time to time.

When you are satisfied that the work is complete, again stand some distance away and consider how best it can be presented. If you have made a garment or useful object, this aspect is likely to have been visualised from the start. There is technical information about making up a wall-hanging and a variety of suggestions for the presentation of a panel in Chapter 7. Think carefully about the alternatives before making your decision.

Finally, in considering the finished work, you can think about pursuing the ideas further in another piece or even a series. Will you exhibit your embroidery?

JUDGING THE WORK

Putting your embroidery up on the wall and looking at it critically should become a regular feature of the way in which you work. Each decision you make is based on your own judgement of what you have already done and on how you can further develop your ideas and intentions. By means of this process you are becoming increasingly sensitive and aware of the many aspects involved in designing and making a piece of work, which inevitably affects the way in which you look at the work of others.

When visiting art galleries, exhibitions, craft shows, etc, people often react to things in terms of 'I like this; I don't care for that' and pass on to the next piece. However, if we spend longer and go round the exhibition again, this time looking much more carefully, we might begin to ask ourselves why

we respond as we do to these different pieces. This is where our knowledge, gained from experience, will come into play.

We could begin by thinking about the subject-matter or content. The soft greens, the sheep and the horizontal lines of the fields give a feeling of calm, while the dark and jagged shapes of the rocky mountain pass seem aggressive and disturbing. Life is not always beautiful, so why should art confine itself to that alone? Art, drama, music and literature all deal at times with the profound emotions, not just the comfortable ones. In being receptive to the unfamiliar we open up new worlds of ideas for ourselves.

These are some of the qualities that are worth looking for in any pieces of art or craftwork:

1 **Imagination** Is it an interesting and personal piece of work, inventive, unusual and original, or just another reiteration of some well-worn theme?

2 **Expressive quality** Does it have something to 'say' (which can apply to a beautiful cushion cover, and not just to a picture)? Do you respond with pleasure and examine it closely, or will you have forgotten about it by the time you leave the gallery?

3 **Use of interesting form** Line, colour, texture, etc. Do you keep noticing, for instance, shapes and colours that relate to each other, or lines that lead the eye to some special point of interest? Do these features enhance the quality of the work?

4 **Craftsmanship** Are the fabrics and threads well handled and is the piece well-made? Is the way it has been worked really lively and exciting?

Bushey Park, drawing by Peter Lees

Competition

Once you begin to take a serious interest in embroidery a certain degree of competition becomes inevitable. If you take an examination in the subject you lay yourself open to the risk of not getting a top mark. If you submit work for a selected exhibition, you accept the possibility of rejection, so must decide whether you are tough enough to contend with the hazard. Remember, though, that your piece might have been the wrong size or colour to fit in with the rest of the work, so have another go next year. Once you have got a certain amount of success 'under your belt', it becomes easier to accept an occasional rejection. Surely by the time a piece of work is finished the best thing is to feel pride and satisfaction that you have sustained the momentum and achieved a conclusion – and then move on to the next project!

STYLE IN EMBROIDERY

Style changes with the world we live in, reflecting and influencing our attitudes and aspirations. Other, more practical, aspects also have bearing, such as the types of materials available at a particular time.

In the sixties and seventies embroiderers began to explore new types of subject-matter, to analyse form in a new way, to experiment with all sorts of materials, to look at traditional methods of embroidery and evolve fresh approaches to their development. The work produced was often abstract in character; it was an exciting and creative period.

At this time the shops were full of wonderful arrays of reasonably cheap fabrics, both natural and synthetic. Dressmaking classes were very popular and everyone had all kinds of materials and scraps stored away in plastic bags. It seemed very logical to enjoy these by building up great collages in which velvet, wool, rayon, nylon, lurex fabrics, cottons and silks were arranged to give contrasts of texture and gradation of colour. Net was popular and this refined the changes in colour even further. People used beads and sequins to emphasise aspects in their designs and trapunto quilting to add a three-dimensional quality to their work.

By the mid seventies however, fabrics were becoming more expensive and there was a trend towards working on calico or silk backgrounds. In response to new movements in the art world the more figurative and pictorial image was returning. During the last ten years further new trends have appeared. Patchwork and quilting are very popular, so there are plenty of cotton fabrics available, but, with the decline in dressmaking, fabric collage is less popular.

This change in materials has meant rethinking our methods – many people now obtain their colour by using fabric dyes of different types, either painted, discharge-printed or spray-painted, etc, plus exquisite scraps of material enriched with closely machined textures and free hand stitching.

Some embroiderers are using fabrics and stitchery in a manner inspired by the French Impressionists, others are concerned with rich textural work. Julia Caprara's panel *Step to Freedom* was inspired by an exhibition brief on the theme 'No more than a Foot'.

> I began to think of measurements, then realised I was much aware of the ground beneath our feet. The surfaces and patterns on paving-stones in London – grey, cracked and often dangerous. I conceived the idea of 'stepping stones' and learning to tread care-

Cloud studies made at
Aberdovey by Elizabeth Ashurst

Step to Freedom by Julia Caprara was inspired by the exhibition brief, 'No more than a foot', and thought of stepping stones. It is worked using layered fabrics and stitched with coton à broder.
12in (30.5cm) square

fully in the flotsam and tide of City life. My work is always symbolic so I realised I was planning a series of stepping-stones through life – 'Steps to Freedom'. Because this was a positive, life-enhancing path, I chose clear jewel-like colours to focus the eye and concentrate the mind.

The panel is worked using fabrics layered across each other and stitched with a coton à broder. These were mounted on fine canvas using tent stitch in strong optical colours. The thickness of yarn and choice of stitch was governed by the need both to contrast and complement neighbouring areas of embroidery, giving a variety of forms and surfaces for the eye to move between.

Many boundaries are down; Barbara Siedlecka, whose initial training was in graphics, will use bleach, boot polish and paint along with fabrics and threads in order to achieve the desired effects. People now use their methods and materials in whatever way they choose in order to express their ideas, thus producing exciting work with the look of today.

Felt-making and paper-making offer interesting and innovative possibilities; rag-rug techniques, perhaps using a rich array of dyed silks, can give lovely effects. Fibre Art is another group which shows very innovative work using fabrics and threads, but not necessarily stitchery, and knitting has returned with a flourish.

CHAPTER 5

ASPECTS OF DESIGN

SHAPE

What do we mean by the term *shape?* Suppose you are sketching or taking a photograph, you are immediately beginning to relate what you see to the shape which will contain it, probably a rectangle. Sometimes, when you are sitting down, practise selecting various pictures from your environment, both the expected things like trees and plants, but also the corners of furniture, the pattern of sunlight, shadows on the ceiling etc. Cut a rectangular 'window' out of a postcard and hold it before your eyes. When you have found an interesting picture, keep moving the 'window' this way and that, up and down, until you have got the placing just right, then ask yourself why this is so and how the shapes of objects relate to each other within the frame. Have you chosen a symmetrical arrangement, or does a large shape seem to be balanced by several smaller ones? Do the negative shapes between the objects have importance? This is the essence of looking and is a habit you will gradually acquire.

Shapes can either be flat or three-dimensional. One's body has shape, as does a piece of sculpture. In both cases we often look at the outline silhouette and observe how this alters as we change our position. If we stand in front of a full-length mirror and move about, some positions look more interesting than others. Try standing with your weight on one foot and notice how the hip line slants and the shoulder line counterbalances by sloping in the opposite direction. A vertical line upwards from the foot that is taking the weight would have different shapes on either side of it, but they must be equal in weight or you would fall over; so here is an example

Echoing Shapes by Jean Colgan

Filham House by Barbara Siedlecka

157

of balanced shapes. A more obvious balance, of course, is the symmetrical one, with feet together and hands by your sides. However, you have only to turn sideways, even in this position, for symmetry to disappear in favour of asymmetrical balance once more.

In designing, shapes read in relation to each other and to the area they occupy. Try to look at them in an abstract way, analysing their qualities and organising them in such a way that they do what you want them to do. Later on, in the process of making the embroidery, you will be considering aspects such as expressive meaning, but just now it is the structure, the strength of the form, direction of line and harmony or tension between shapes that must be achieved. Indeed, this is very much part of the expressive meaning.

Quite often we find shapes that echo each other, or we organise our design to make this happen. If shapes seem to 'bump' each other, they can feel quite uncomfortable and aggressive, so they will need to be moved unless you specifically want this effect.

In working with shapes on a background, the negative areas, or spaces between, are very important. It is wise to keep the shapes fairly close together so they seem to belong to each other. If the background area between them is greater than the shapes themselves, they lose significance. Why not try playing with a 'family of shapes'?

A family of shapes

If you have worked through some of the exercises in Chapter 1 you may have built up a collage by cutting various shapes and sizes of rectangles from fabrics in one range of colour and arranging them on a background. You may also have designed a panel using a silhouette-shape of a leaf or piece of fruit in three sizes and another one based on drawings of car wheels initially cut out of paper and overlapped. In Chapter 2 there is a section on lettering cut directly from folded paper and another one in which paper strips or circles are folded, cut and arranged to make patterns. Each of these exercises

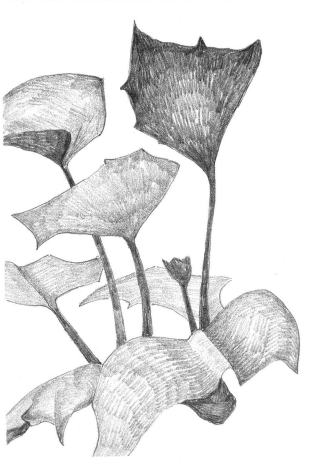

Plant sketches by Gordon Faulkner, showing the flexibility of leaf shapes

Umbrellas by Jean Colgan –
using a familiar shape to create
a new design

Jean Colgan's sketches of a cane
and bead curtain have led to an
idea for a design using long
straight stitches (below left)

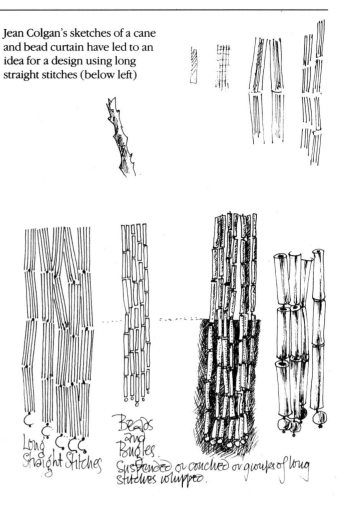

has been based on a 'family of shapes', ie, shapes that are similar but different from each other, and has been carried out by the direct 'hands on' method of designing by cutting directly without drawing first. Can we extend these possibilities further?

Let us now look for examples of similar but varied shapes in nature. Blown autumn leaves from the same tree will display like patterns of growth, but the Stag's Horn Sumach (*Rhus typhina*), for example, sheds leaves which range in colour from green to gold and to brilliant red. Their long slender shapes make patterns as they fall on the grass, lying across each other in every direction. Look through cupped hands to isolate the most inspiring area. Beech and hosta leaves, on the other hand, curl into quite amazing forms which could offer a challenge for a three-dimensional design.

Pause, too, to notice everyday kitchen images – a bowlful of sliced leeks; white, pale yellow to deep green, some in whole rings, others floating arcs, creating a rich all-over pattern.

Machine-made objects offer a similar wealth of possibilities. Shapes can be simplified and formalised so that the pattern is significant, rather than the subject-matter. Certain lines can be eliminated to create new shapes but, as they started from the same source, they must surely maintain their comfortable relationship with each other. Have you ever thought of drawing a box full of miscellaneous buttons, a jar of screws or curtain rings, a bag of rubber bands? Imagine a close-up

photographic slide of any of these thrown up very large on a screen. If this were a sheet of paper on the wall, you could draw round some of the shapes – food for thought!

The patterns discussed so far are random, but many packaged goods make neat and orderly patterns. Sets of screwdrivers, rows of zip fasteners on a stand, packets of coloured stationery, displays of lipsticks and boxes of eyeshadow fit into this category.

Let us consider another way of designing from small objects such as a pencil sharpener, a buckle, a clothes peg, a plastic bottle top. Draw the object from the front, back, top, bottom and sides.

The diagram below shows the variety of shapes offered by a pencil sharpener. They are related because they are parts of the same object. Shapes could be cut out of different papers, in different sizes, as before, and pushed about on a contrasting background to produce all kinds of varied patterns. These could be random or formal, border patterns suitable for dress embroidery, a series of designs for a set of cushion covers or a large abstract wall-hanging etc. Add to that the possibilities offered by a great variety of methods – you could be busy!

Shapes from a pencil sharpener

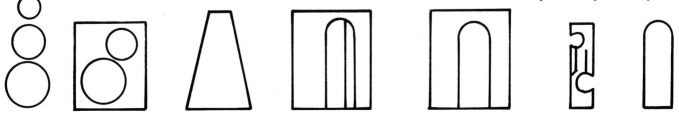

Exploring a repeat design:
hearts

Experimenting with cut and
'exploded' shapes

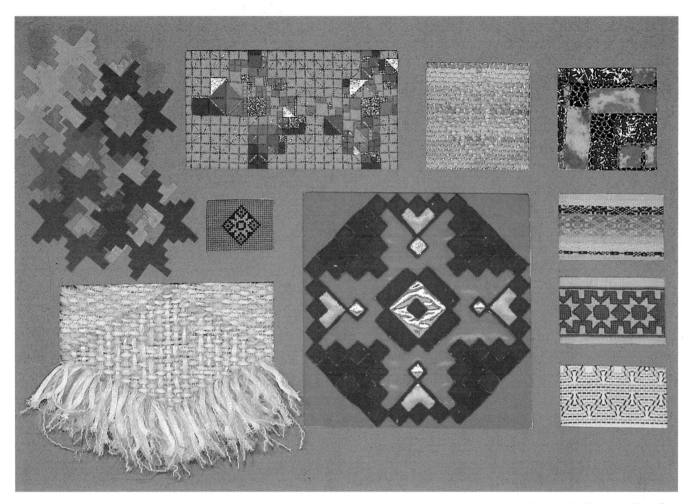

PATTERN

Clothing has been decorated with embroidery from the earliest times and, although fashions come and go, most people enjoy wearing something special and individual. Embroidery in its many forms can be used on collars, cuffs, pockets, borders on jackets, skirts, etc, for children's clothes, hats and so on. It is also often used on household objects, including table-cloths, mats, cushions, decorative boxes, bags of various kinds, quilts, etc.

The design for a repeating pattern needs to relate to the materials, the methods of working and the shape of the garment or object that is to be decorated. This will produce a feeling of 'rightness'; decoration is a means of extending and completing an idea, but take care not to overdo it.

Many aspects of pattern-making are interesting and invite us to be inventive and innovative. How should we set about producing lively designs of our own?

Some ways of building up repeating patterns

A repeating pattern is normally built up from one or more simplified shapes, sometimes referred to as motifs, or just as units, that are put together in various ways. The diagram opposite explores the ways in which one simple unit can be repeated and the designs that result. If you use two shapes, or several, the scope is obviously tremendous. The next question is 'What shape shall I choose'?

Suggestions for starting points

a Having just worked with a heart shape try clubs, spades and diamonds.

Pattern by Margaret Chandler. Design sheet based on an Indian textile. *26 x 16½in (66 x 42cm)*

b In the previous section, a way is shown of producing a number of different shapes from one object, a pencil sharpener, and suggestions made of other small man-made objects that might be useful. Examine a brooch, or other piece of jewellery.

c Natural form. Leaves and flowers have always been used, but perhaps you can find something unusual. The seed-head of a poppy, or wings of a sycamore tree; a starfish, fruit or vegetable, etc, but remember to keep the shape simple and interesting – you will have plenty of scope for detail when you come to the stitching.

d Cut and 'explode' a geometric shape such as a square, circle, rectangle or cross, spread the pieces apart and stick them on to a contrasting background of paper. There are many variations on this theme too, as the sketches show.

e Look at road-signs, logos, symbols.

f Patterns can also be created directly on the fabrics using stitches, ribbons, beads, etc. See Chapter 1, exercise 3, in which a way to solve the problem of corners is explained.

In Margaret Chandler's design sheet (illustrated), a motif from an Indian textile was chosen as a starting point and the pattern explored and developed, using a range of different techniques.

Chinese Dragon

Space filling

Sometimes we need to create a design within a particular shape, eg a lion on a shield for a banner or, in my example, a Chinese dragon to fill a specified but irregular shape for a floor mosaic.

How can we position it successfully? First draw out the shape to be filled quite accurately on paper, then draw an equal margin all round within it. For the dragon this was quite narrow, but do consider the width very carefully. Design within the smaller area, arranging to touch it at fairly regular intervals, eg the head and the tongue, the claws, tail and so on. Look really critically at the spaces lying between the out-stretched parts of the body; are they well-balanced overall? How does the surface area covered by the creature compare with the background; would it be better if there were more background space? You might have to enlarge or reduce the size of the beast, or thicken its limbs or thin it down, but now is the time to get it right. When you are satisfied, rub out the margin which was just a guideline.

LINE

Chapter 1 commenced with a few exercises using line as a starting point for exploring simple stitches. Let us give further consideration to the meaning and function of this term.

Line is an abstract quality of design, closely related to shape; for instance, by joining up several lines you can create a shape of which the edges may be very significant in your design. Let us think about lines and consider how varied and expressive they can be.

Arrows are used as road signs and general directions because they are instantly comprehensible, even when the message is quite complex. A system of lines is painted on the roads themselves to tell us when we can overtake, when we must stop and give way, and so on. Roads and railways carve sweeping lines across the countryside, and aeroplanes make vapour trails in the sky.

Line is a term also used in fashion – we can look at old photographs and virtually date them by the particular 'line' of the time – the short skirts and Eton-crop haircuts of the 1920s, for example.

Line is just as significant in architecture – arches, vaulting and flowing curves. In the post-war period there has been much emphasis on high-rise buildings, vertical and horizontal lines and rectangular forms.

Line features also in the crafts; in furniture, wrought-iron work, jewellery, to name just a few. William Morris' block-printed fabrics have strong linear rhythms based on natural form and these make very satisfying repeats, reading well from a distance.

Nature is full of linear forms, in rock formations, waterfalls, growth of plants and trees, etc.

RHYTHM AND MOVEMENT IN DESIGN

We all know what is meant in practice by the terms 'rhythm' and 'movement', but it is less easy to explain them in words. In the dictionary rhythm is described mainly in terms of music, but these aspects are at the heart of all successful pieces of embroidery.

Nature is full of rhythms, such as day and night, the sun and the moon, the seasons, the life cycle of plants and animals, the human heart-beat, flow of blood, etc. In science all sorts of rhythms are recognised and measured. The electrocardiogram is a graphic representation of natural rhythms.

Liza Pembroke has produced an admirable example of the use of rhythm in her panel *Flashes of Light* (overleaf). She felt her design needed to be dramatic in order to convey the life threatening nature of stress. Florentine work seemed to offer just the right method for expressing these ideas and the colours were chosen for their symbolic meaning:

> The purple background – purple synonymous with sensuality, ecclesiastical symbolism; a rich and passionate colour, very much the colour of life
> Red – blood, the heart, fire, aggression
> Pinks – warm, 'in the pink'
> Orange – an earth colour, glows as in a fire, energy
> Yellow – sunshine, joy, a happy colour, plants of springtime – daffodils, crocus, new life and hope.

(The colour references were taken from *Colour* Leisure Books, 1988.)

To increase the dramatic effect lines of paint were carried across the black mounting boards.

The world of the machine is highly dependent on the related movements of different parts, on a huge scale, or on the small scale of the domestic sewing-machine.

Nature is full of linear forms –
note the growth of this plant

We encounter rhythm in the beating of a drum, the tapping of fingers and of footsteps. We can watch or participate in dancing, swimming, skating, games and athletics, horse-riding, etc, and observe the activities of birds, frogs, cats, bees, etc, where the movements are flowing, rhythmic, repetitive and varied. We can also recognise rhythm and movement in landscape, the growth of plants and perhaps even in the way we arrange our furniture. These things create feelings and responses of interest, pleasure, comfort, etc. These daily associations in every aspect of our lives will naturally find expression in the visual arts and crafts.

The feeling of rhythm and movement is created by all kinds of flowing lines, which perhaps repeat with variations and by the repetition of shapes that echo each other; these may include jagged, zigzagged or spiralling forms, etc. The eye can be led inwards towards a focal point, or outward from it, by the use of lines and also be encouraged to move across a piece of work by the use of tone and colour.

A PROJECT IN LINE, RHYTHM AND MOVEMENT

Here are some suggestions that might help you to develop your observation and awareness of line, rhythm and movement, both in a practical way and by researching this area more fully.

Road signs inspired this
drawing by Peter Lees

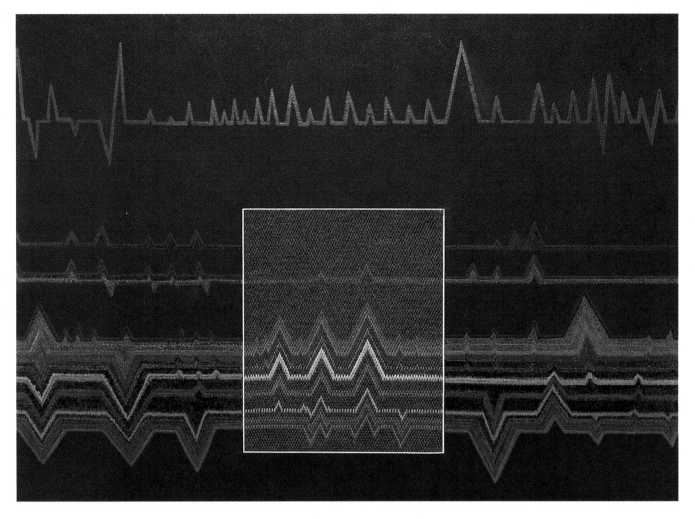

1   Once again, think of some words that describe different types of line, such as flowing, radiating, criss-cross, spiralling, etc. Try to express the quality of your word by drawing with two or three pencils or coloured pens held firmly together. If you use a layout pad you could overlay two of your designs to produce a third one; if the lines are hard to see, press your papers against a window pane and move them around to get the best results.

2   Again with some special linear quality in mind, lay a rich pattern of lines in varying thicknesses of string on a piece of card, possibly adding a coloured one as well. Stick them all in place using a firm adhesive.

This exercise could be further extended by inking up your block with lino-printing ink and a roller and printing it on paper or a smooth fabric, either singly or to create several repeating patterns.

3   The sculptor Henry Moore evolved a way of drawing using contour lines which 'feel' their way across a form and produced work which had a sense of great solidity. Try doing your own contour drawing of a pebble, a piece of driftwood, a knobbly Jerusalem artichoke, or the folds in a piece of fabric, using a pen with a fairly fine point. You may find that you produce quite a naturalistic image, or something rather abstract.

4   Lines can imply movement or stability. Look at paintings by for example, Botticelli, Matisse, Toulouse-Lautrec, or one of the Futurists, and notice how the feeling of flow, running through a figure from an outstretched hand to the back foot, can often be expressed by a single line. Buy an art postcard and, after placing some layout or tracing paper over it, analyse

Flashes of Life by Liza Pembroke. This piece of Florentine embroidery is based on the recording of an electrocardiogram. *24 x 16¹⁄₂ (61 x 42cm)*

Sea and Sky: an example of drawing with an eraser, by Susan Wells

Rhythmic lines of string on card

The human body, the ultimate
expression of flowing lines

the movement by drawing in the main lines of the picture. Try this too with landscape, either from paintings or from your own photographs, and then mount your pictures and the analysis of them side by side. They will remind you to look at paintings in this way when next you visit an art gallery. Can you find examples of stability too?

5   Find some newspaper pictures of sport, such as tennis, football, horse-racing, or of animals running, jumping, etc, and analyse these in a similar fashion. Again, draw the lines which seem most significant; sometimes they will be the general flow through a figure and sometimes an outline of the form; you will know which to select.

6   Make notes, sketches and collect pictures of architecture and related ornament that interests you. This might involve visiting a museum or library, or it could become the focus of a holiday, perhaps to study the work of Scottish architect Charles Rennie Mackintosh in Glasgow, or to see the decorated domes of St Basil's Cathedral in Moscow, the exuberence of Viennese Baroque fountains or the new buildings at Docklands in East London.

   Perhaps your explorations will suggest a new direction for your embroidery, either now or in the future.

COLOUR

In Chapter 1, we looked at a simple colour circle, noting the three primary colours (yellow, red and blue) and how, by mixing them together in turn, the secondary colours (orange, purple and green) are produced. We also carried out an exercise in which the use of complementary or opposite colours was explored.

   Some people find it helpful to paint their own colour circle, using a standard yellow, red and blue, ie, the particular colours which, when mixed together, should give the best possible secondary colours. In carrying out this exercise, it is

Jean Colgan's design of athletes
was taken from a newspaper
cutting, first tracing over the
important lines

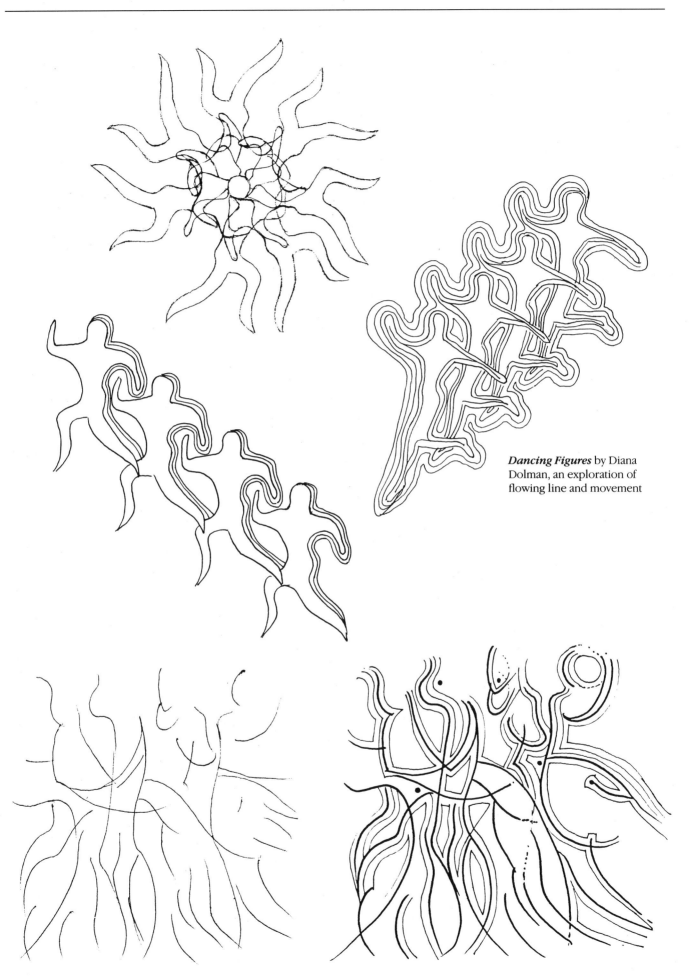

Dancing Figures by Diana Dolman, an exploration of flowing line and movement

Fields of Fire by Elizabeth Ashurst. This work expresses the embroiderer's concern with the threat of technology to the environment and its consequent effects on ecology. Strips of hand-dyed fabrics and perlé threads are used *56¹/₂ x 34in (143 x 86cm)*

Colour circle

worthwhile extending the colour circle further to include the tertiaries, by mixing every two adjacent colours as shown in the diagram below; this will produce a more subtle grading. Poster colour or gouache is the appropriate medium to use and keep the paint thick, with little or no water added. Try to make an equal mixture of the two colours in every instance.

As no black or white is added to these colours, they are of full 'intensity', a term referring to a colour's strength and purity.

Here are some other terms used in reference to colour.

Analogous   These are any group of adjacent colours in the colour circle, eg greens through blues to purple, which can produce a pleasing and harmonious scheme, especially when the tonal variations are added.

Warm and cold   Warm colours are those associated with heat, the reds, oranges and yellows, while the cold colours are the greens, blues and purples. Warm colours generally appear to come forward while cold ones seem to recede.

Discordant   In the colour circle yellow is the lightest colour, orange and green a little darker, red and blue darker still and purple darkest of all. If you reverse this order, for instance by adding black to yellow to make a khaki or green colour, and if white is added to purple to make a mauve that is paler than the khaki, the result will give a 'kick' (or vibrant quality) which may be useful in giving importance to a focal point, but can be very puzzling if you achieve it by accident. When you understand what is happening you can emphasise or eliminate it as you feel the need.

A colour exercise

In order to discover more about colour relationships, you might enjoy tackling the following painting exercise.

Materials required

Poster colour or gouache in two complementary colours, eg blue and orange, and black and white

Paintbrushes

A palette

Cartridge paper

A rag or kitchen paper for wiping brushes

Be sure, as usual, to keep your paint solid and opaque.

The aim is to mix various proportions of

1 Orange and white
  Orange and black
  Orange, white and black

2 Blue and white
  Blue and black
  Blue, white and black

3 Orange and blue
  Orange, blue and white
  Orange, blue and black
  Orange, blue, white and black

As you produce your various mixtures of colour, paint out an area of about 2in (5cm) square in each. You will be surprised at the enormous variety of colours that you produce.

When you get tired of painting, cut or tear out each of your units of colour and then play with them on a fresh sheet of paper, trying out all sorts of colour and tonal combinations. As they all come from the same source, they must relate, mustn't they? When you have arrived at a result you like, stick them all down.

If you carried out the same exercise with red and green, or purple and yellow, you would then have some very useful

(above)
Spring into Summer – Early spring (detail)

(below)
Spring into Summer – Late summer (detail)

reference sheets to help with planning colour schemes in the future.

Colours seem to change according to their context, as you may have discovered already from the exercise above, or by laying different fabrics side by side and noticing how they work together. Constance Howard's panel *Squares and Stripes* (page 6) illustrates this point very well.

> One of my interests in wrapping these panels is to show depth, with graduated areas of colours or with sharp contrasts of tone. Narrow horizontal stripes in bright colour against greyed colour give vitality, while light against dark pattern gives an illusion of roundness.

> The technique is limited to geometric shapes. I use perlé cottons, numbers eight, five or three according to the design and size of the wrapping. This is worked over inch or half-inch strips of card which are assembled and glued to a card backing.

> The design is worked out in detail on graph paper, usually in tonal values first of all, then in colour, but my ideas often develop further when I commence wrapping the threads.

> This particular piece was number five perlé cotton throughout, with strips one inch in width.

Colour can also have an emotional meaning; what colours do you associate with anger, mourning, springtime, tranquillity?

In her panel *Fields of Fire* (page 168) Elizabeth Ashurst is making a strong statement of her views on the rapidly increasing threat of technology to the environment and its consequent effects on ecology. She illustrates the burning of straw and stubble in autumn and the air pollution and destruction of wildlife that this causes.

The design, based on sketches made in Lincolnshire, is worked with perlé threads and strips of hand-dyed silks and cottons into a canvas ground with upright gobelin stitches. Two meshes of canvas are used, the finer of 10 threads to the inch (2.5cm) and the other of 5 threads. The intensity of the colour she uses helps to express her feelings on this matter.

Colour was the theme of the Elvin Hall wall hangings, based on the four seasons. There were two large hangings, *Spring into Summer* (page 169) and *Autumn into Winter*, each 17ft 6in x 6ft (5.34 x 1.84m) and four small ones.

Log cabin patchwork units in six sizes were made in rich-looking rayon dupion fabrics with velvet or corduroy centres and applied to a screen-printed background of calico, quite a contrast. The largest one was 3ft (91.5cm) square and the smallest just 2in (5cm). The printed design was a repeat of a 10in (25.5cm) square, which left spaces into which the standard patchwork units fitted. The colour of the print changed subtly in each of the five fabric widths, sometimes it was printed vertically and sometimes horizontally.

I wanted to create a feeling of movement across the design from left to right and devised several means of achieving it. The velvet centres changed colour; I worked across from the cold yellows of daffodils in spring to the peach, orange and red of summer and on to the mauves and bronze of Michaelmas daisies and chrysanthemums in autumn. Touches of cold pink and blue were used here and there to carry the eye across the panel. A change was also made from the calm horizontals, to a vertical use of the light and dark halves of the squares to give a dynamic emphasis to high summer, while moving towards the largest square and main feature in the design. The colours in the horizontal borders changed too.

A group of friends helped with the enormous task of making up the six panels.

Returning now to the colour circle, we should also recognise its limitations. It leaves out the range of turquoise and sea-greens, the cyclamen and puce pinks and the yellow ochres; these colours cannot be mixed from the red, yellow and blue primary colours. In working once with a group of analogous colours from red, through puce to violet and purple, I had difficulty in bringing this scheme to life until a light, bright orange was added. This gave the necessary touch of magic. The particular lightness was a surprise and our usual, perhaps simple, colour theory did not explain why this should be. Nevertheless, the colour circle does help us to understand and use colour and also helps in the search for a colour to fulfil a particular purpose.

Some people always prefer to start from a painting or coloured sketch, enjoying translating this into materials and perhaps painting some of the areas with fabric dyes and inks; others prefer the hands-on method of working out a colour scheme in the actual fabrics and threads: a ready-made palette of colour. In this way the textural qualities of the particular materials can be taken into account. There is no 'correct' way of working – it is a matter of personal inclination.

Sometimes, of course, it is necessary to present a painted design when working to commission. In this case it is advisable to add a proviso that the colours may change slightly in the finished work, according to the availability of materials and the demands of the design itself.

TONE VALUE

When using the terms 'tone value' or 'tone', we are referring to the lightness or darkness of a colour. This can be recognised quite easily within a single colour range, but not so readily in relating different colours to each other. In order to understand more fully what is meant by 'tone', you may find it helpful to carry out the following exercise:

Materials required
> White, red and black poster paint, or gouache
> Some paintbrushes and a palette or white plate
> Some cartridge paper
> A rag or kitchen paper for wiping the brushes
> *Method*

Mark out three bands of ¾in (2cm) squares on your paper, with nine squares in each band and a space between them, as shown in the diagram.

When mixing the colours, make sure that your paint remains solid and opaque throughout the exercise.

1 Paint the left-hand square (a) of each band in white and the right-hand square (i) in black.

Return now to the first row. Add a little black to the white to produce a pale grey and paint square (b). Carry on doing this, square by square, adding a little more black each time. Aim to achieve an even range of tones, becoming gradually darker until you arrive at black. The middle square (e) should therefore be an equal mixture of black and white. This is not particularly easy; you may need to overpaint some of your squares until you are satisfied with the progression of tones. It is useful to try out the paint on the edge of a spare piece of paper and match it up to check that you have got it right before you repaint.

2 Start as before, on the second band of squares, this time

adding a little red to the white and working across from the palest pink to the centre square (e) which will be pure red. This range of pinks is traditionally known as the 'tints'.

Now begin adding black to the pure red, and continue grading your tones carefully until you reach the black. These are known as the 'shades'.

3 Starting off again on the third band of squares, mix an equal amount of black and red, add a little of this mixture to the white and keep going until you get to black.

4 Cut out your three strips of graded tones, then lay them side by side and check that the grey, the pink and the pinky-grey below it are all exactly of the same tone. It may be necessary to make adjustments,even at this stage, until you are satisfied that this is the case across all the strips.

It is interesting that in the middle we find a grey, a pure red and a muted pinky-grey that are of identical tone value. They may be uncomfortable to look at, as they seem to 'jump' a bit. Try sliding one to the right, one to the left and so on, and see how they relate to each other, then reverse them and note the effect. How much variety there is, even in this limited colour scheme! If you wanted to achieve a strong and dynamic effect in your embroidery, which tones would you use together? There is also the question of how large in area a particular tone should be.

Keep your strips and, if you wish to pursue this further, you might be able to obtain strips of graded tones in different colours from a painting and decorating shop.

Once you have come to understand how tones work together, you will usually resolve questions of tone value in the materials themselves by laying fabrics and threads side by

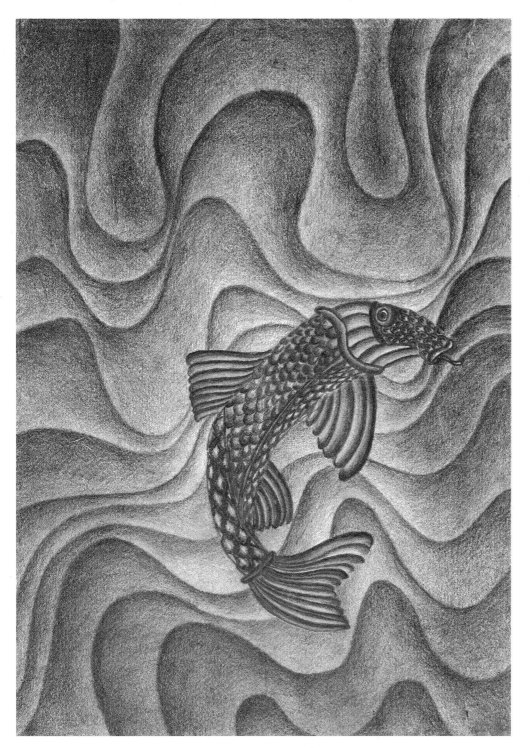

Fish by Charlotte Lees

Tone value: bands of squares

Exercise 1

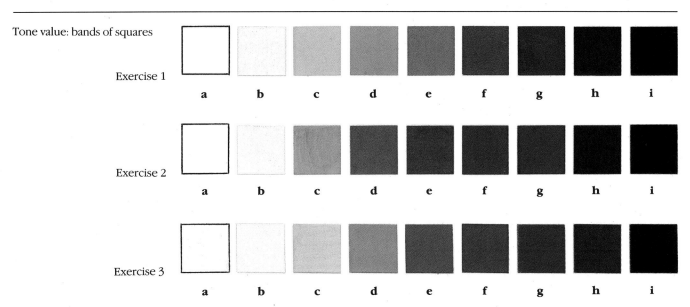

a b c d e f g h i

Exercise 2

a b c d e f g h i

Exercise 3

a b c d e f g h i

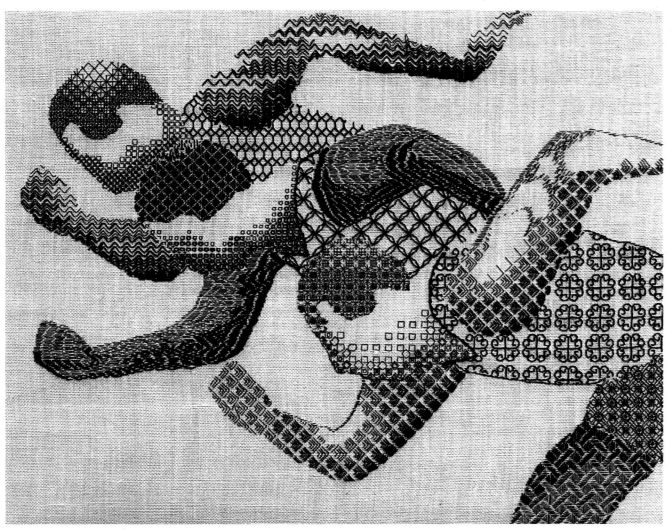

Black for Gold by Gill Pickup.
A blackwork panel worked at
the time of the Olympics.
15¹/₂ x 12in (39 x 30cm)

Twilight by Marion Mitchell. A
richly textural piece worked on
three different scales of canvas.
22 x 26in (56 x 66cm)

side. Planning and positioning them is a more difficult problem, but this can often be dealt with by trial and error. Generally speaking, unequal areas of tone or colour work better than equal ones and darker tones seem more comfortable at the base.

Another aspect of tone in relation to embroidery is the effect of light on fabrics and threads. Shiny fabrics reflect the light, while opaque ones absorb it. As 'shot' fabrics change direction, their tone values vary and, as we discovered in Chapter 1, exercise 7, this applies also in the use of shiny threads in stitchery. Raised stitches and padded areas create shadows and the density of stitches also changes the tonal effect.

Blackwork

Blackwork is a traditional embroidery method which depends almost entirely on the qualities of tone and texture. In this method, tiny all-over patterns are counted and stitched into an evenweave fabric, usually white or cream. Variety of tone can be achieved by variation in the thickness of threads, the density of the patterns, or the development of a simple pattern into a more complicated one, and by making good use of the contrasting background areas. Designs can be planned by cutting up newspapers, making a collage of the different densities of tone and relating the stitches to match them.

Gill Pickup's panel *Black for Gold* (page 172) was inspired by work on tonal exercises in life-classes and the exploration of Blackwork embroidery that she was doing at the time of the Olympics.

> The intermingling of shapes, the variety of skin tones, changes of density of stitching and varied thread thickness and lustre fascinated me in its complexity in this portrayal of sport.
>
> I believe there were too many conflicting problems for the piece to be wholly successful, but I learned a great deal from its execution.

TEXTURE

Texture is a most enjoyable and sensuous aspect of embroidery involving both visual and tactile experiences – looking and seeing, touching and feeling – as we select and use our materials. The term 'texture' refers both to the inherent surface qualities of fabrics and threads and to the effects that can be achieved by their use.

Fabrics have an innate look and feel of their own. They vary according to the materials from which they are made, how they are spun and how they are woven. Fabrics can be rough, firm, coarse, shiny and reflective of light, etc. Some are very soft and smooth, while others have a varied surface due to the use of a 'slub' thread of uneven thickness inserted into the weft. 'Shot' fabrics have a different colour in warp and weft and appear to change colour according to the direction in which they lie, especially if they are also shiny. Knitted fabrics stretch and the surface will differ in character from that of woven fabrics. Organzas can have a delicate shimmering surface, as do the very fine metallic fabrics that are being produced now. Leathers of different types can also add textural quality to a piece of work.

Threads vary likewise, ranging from fine to thick, soft to stiff, etc, and may be of differing 'ply' (the number of threads twisted together). They can be fluffy or knobbly, silky or hairy and there are many interesting knitting threads available which consist of mixtures of wool, cotton, silk, synthetics, etc, with perhaps each strand varying in colour and texture. It might be difficult to stitch with such threads, but they can be laid or couched on the surface of a design. Very shiny and metallic threads offer further possibilities and many of these are now obtainable, some made specifically for use on the sewing-machine, including variegated threads in a number of attractive colour ranges. There are also metal threads made specially for goldwork and particularly used in ecclesiastical embroidery.

The other aspect of texture is the way in which the materials are used. The qualities of fabrics can be contrasted with each other or emphasised by the use of padding and quilting. The fabrics can be laid flat on a background; they can also be pleated, ruched, bunched up or used in tiny snippets, built up in layers, torn, unravelled, hacked with scissors, etc, as we have discovered in the section on the manipulation of fabrics, threads and other materials in Chapter 2 and in people's descriptions of how they work.

'Texture' is a term particularly applicable to the use of all kinds of stitchery in which the size and direction of the stitches, their thickness or flatness, the knotted or looped

Bird by Jean Colgan, an excellent design for textured embroidery

qualities, etc, can be contrasted, developed and exploited.

Pat Bright's canvaswork panel *Grasses* (page 176) is a good example of this:

> This piece has taken many, many hours of thought and stitching. I wanted to achieve the graceful flowing curves of ornamental grasses, some in bud and some in full flower. As canvas is a squared medium to work on, this was more difficult than first envisaged. I wanted the grasses to flow and have movement and to stand away from the background. (Some fabrics were included to obtain a larger variety of texture.)

Marion Mitchell has also combined the use of canvaswork with fabrics in her panel *Twilight* (page 173), another texturally rich piece. The embroiderer has selected her materials and stitches with care in order to express her ideas and feelings:

> My love of canvaswork and the textures which can be achieved, along with a passion for colour, was the starting point for this panel. I had collected a variety of textured yarns in black, including one with a multi-coloured lurex thread through it, which glinted like points of light in darkness. I wanted to contrast textures – smooth, hairy, shiny, glittering – within an inky black colour scheme punctuated by points of bright luminous colour.
>
> The panel was constructed in three layers and three different scales of canvas – from the rug canvas in the foreground to the fine canvas of the 'horizon'.
>
> The stitches were chosen for their ability to merge and blend with one another – chevron, eyelet, cushion, French and bullion knots. The texture was accentuated by couched cords and ruched ribbons.
>
> The end result suggested a darkening sky with a luminous horizon and a dense shadowy foreground.

Beads, sequins, cords and ribbons can be added to intensify the rich effect of stitchery. Threads can be used in fringes, hand-made cords, or left as uncut ends to hang, dangle or float across a piece of work.

Is it surprising that embroidery is such a fascinating field in which to work when so many different qualities are on offer? It is great fun to play with such an Aladdin's Cave of delightful possibilities, but it is also very easy to be seduced by such rich and delicious materials. We must learn when to stop; it is necessary to ask oneself such questions as 'What am I trying to say'? and 'Am I expressing an idea that is meaningful to me, or am I being carried away?'

THE FOCAL POINT

Sometimes, when designing, it is useful or necessary to achieve a focal point; ie, some area of special emphasis to which the eye will be drawn. The ancient Greeks, and later the artists of the Renaissance, explored the use of a mathematical formula known as the Golden Section, to produce an ideal proportion and give a visually satisfying focal point that was off-centre, both in the width and the height of the picture. There have been other systems too. Many artists of today, however, tend to work more intuitively and they may or may not use a special centre of interest. If they do, it could well appear in some unexpected and off-beat place in the design to produce a shock of surprise.

If you wish to produce a special focus of emphasis, how can this be achieved? The possibilities are very wide: you can use variations of scale, colour, tone, texture or other visual qualities together or individually. For instance, a small area of intense colour or strongly contrasting tones might be surrounded by areas which gradually increase in size, while the colours become more muted and less dynamic.

A different approach would be to use the largest unit in the design as the focal point. In the wall-hanging *Spring into Summer,* see page 169, a very large log cabin patchwork square has been used in this way and, at the same time, each of the one hundred units in the design has its own focal point of a velvet or corduroy square at its centre.

A focal point could also be padded and encrusted with a rich texture of stitchery, beads, etc, while surrounding areas could be more sparingly stitched. Incidentally, additional but less strong points of emphasis are often useful in linking the whole design together. Another way of emphasising an area is by the use of line and rhythm to lead the eye inwards. Alternatively, the focus can be used as the starting point of the design, from which lines of movement flow outwards.

Not all designs require or use a focal point, but look at the panel *Urban Colours* by Caroline Baker on page 91, in which a small blue square surrounded by various yellows seems to be a focus to the design. Look at other pictures in the book and notice how people have achieved special emphases.

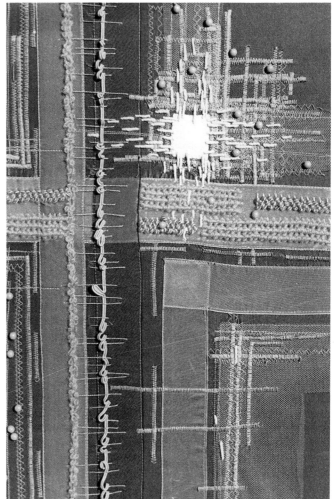

Ribbons, the focal point emphasised with bullion knots. *14 x 16in (36 x 41cm)*

DEPTH

Generally speaking embroidery is not the medium for a very naturalistic representation – it is very difficult to achieve all the nuances obtainable in painting.

To what extent, then, should a feeling of depth be sought after in an embroidery? A side-view of a dog is likely to offer a shapely form and perhaps a feeling of movement, whereas a front view of a seated spaniel would be extremely complicated.

This does not mean, of course, that all design must be confined to a decorative flat pattern. Quite often we see a landscape in which the important feature is the great feeling of distance. We may find that areas appear to recede in a series

of flat, subtle greys, growing gradually lighter, while near areas come forward because we can see much more detail and the colours are stronger and more intense. This is known as 'aerial perspective'. Near things also, of course, appear larger, while a tree or a house in the distance can appear as just a tiny dot. So tone-value, intensity of colour and scale are all involved in this impression of distance, as depicted, for example, in Isabel Mulloy's panel *Lava Moss*:

> While on holiday in Iceland I was fascinated by the moss which covers the lava beds. The colour varies according to the age of the lava it grows on; a photograph of the moss inspired my embroidery. I made a rough sketch as a guide and chose a loose lumpy

Grasses by Pat Bright. A canvas-worked panel using the textural qualities of the medium. *22 x 22½ (56 x 57cm)*

Lava Moss by Isabel Mulloy. This work was inspired by a photograph taken while on holiday in Iceland. It is worked throughout in buttonhole stitch. *9½ x 10in (24 x 25.5cm)*

material to work on as I'd decided to do buttonhole stitch throughout and the combination might help to convey the terrain. A small area of the background material was painted blue as in the photograph, the rest left natural. Threads and wools were chosen as near the colours in the photo as possible.

Buttonhole stitch was worked on the blue area and cottons and wools worked to and fro to simulate the undulations made by the moss on the lava.

Towards the foreground a varied detached buttonhole stitch was introduced to suggest the way the moss overhangs the lava. Knitted pieces were added for the mounds in the foreground.

Traditional perspective, in which lines converge to points on the horizon (ie one's own eye-level) was developed by artists in the early Renaissance to create what we might now call a type of photographic realism. Learning to draw in perspective is a skill of value to a future painter, but of less importance to people working in media other than paint. Many painters of the twentieth century have favoured the 'naive' qualities in children's work and the work of so-called primitive cultures – and have often achieved their effect without using formal perspective at all.

There have been times when I have chosen to make use of formal perspective, as in *Boy with Two Ice-Creams,* though always with the above considerations in mind. Eirian Short, however, takes a different view: her background is in

sculpture and she continues to be interested in the problems of depicting three-dimensional objects on a flat surface. Unlike the 'flat-pattern' school, she aims to make her images as solid and real as possible. See her drawings of *The Morvil Foxes* (page 107), and her panel *Hydrangeas* (page 78), both of which depict this aspect. If you are interested in ways of achieving depth and roundness, it is a good idea to join a life-class.

Side views of a dog, offering form and movement

177

CHAPTER 6

RECORDING AN IMAGE

DRAWING WITH A PENCIL

For many people the term 'drawing' implies working with a pencil and they feel discouraged because it is not an easy tool to use. It can produce very disappointing results in the hands of the timid or unskilled, especially if the pencil is the one in most general use, an HB (Hard Black), which may well produce a thin grey line or, if blunt, a woolly grey one. However, with a certain amount of practice, and with the right equipment to hand, it is possible to improve one's skill quite rapidly.

It is useful to collect a range of pencils: HB, B, 2B, 3B, 4B, 5B, and 6B, and a knife rather than a pencil sharpener for keeping the point long and sharp; this shaping of the point is absolutely essential. Draw on cartridge paper, which has a finely textured surface, and use a drawing-board or piece of hardboard or strong card to rest it on at a comfortable angle, unless you are using a drawing pad.

It is well worth spending time on learning what your pencils will do, by making marks on your paper with each in turn.

This pencil drawing by Charlotte Lees, shows good use of contrasting tone

Let the pencil lie loosely between your thumb and straightened first finger, with about 1½-2in (4-5cm) extending beyond your fingertip and resting on your second finger, then move your arm from the elbow, or from your shoulder, which will give a flowing quality to the lines you make. Try to avoid holding the pencil tightly between thumb and first finger as you would hold it for writing. Draw some long sweeping lines, then produce textures working round and round as you might do in machine embroidery and make groups of lines overlapping each other, like working with straight stitches. See how these work using different pencils and then make a solid area of tone one inch (2cm) square as dark as each pencil permits.

Now have a go at drawing a plant, or some flowers in a vase, working on A4 or, better still, A3-sized paper. Spend some time looking at the plant before you begin, noticing the main lines of the stem and the general outline shape, then rough these in first so that you are really filling the paper. If the lines are not right first time, draw them again until you are satisfied, but leave all the lines in and avoid using a rubber (eraser). Gradually build up your picture, if necessary going up to the plant so that you really understand what is happening. When you have sketched it all in, use your blackest pencil (6B) and draw in all the darkest areas of tone quite solidly; these could be the under-side of a leaf, a shadow, or something dark behind the plant. Then draw in a middle grey and a light grey, leaving the white paper for your highlights. Lay a piece of paper across the work to avoid smudging it with your hand as you draw. How does it look?

Next, try drawing your plant again, but this time in line only. Vary the darkness and thickness of your lines as you draw, either by pressing more heavily, or working with the side of the pencil point as it flows across the paper, again make use of your different pencils. Strong, crisp lines would help make the near lines come forward, while softer and greyer lines might look further away. If you are not pleased with what you have done remember that learning to draw takes time and practice and is rarely an innate talent. Many embroiderers find art classes give valuable experience. Also, if you have the chance, visit an art gallery and look at drawings, or borrow a book which gives examples of drawings by different artists and notice how they make use of line and tone.

DRAWING WITH A PEN

A pen is useful either for making quick notes, sketching, or for more finished work. You can, of course, jot things down quite successfully with an ordinary fountain pen or biro (ball point), and sketch with these too. However, there are now many kinds of pens available at art shops, or stationery stores, that are specially made in varying thickness of nib for drawing

Pen drawing by Jean Colgan, using the hatching technique to give tone

Three Women, a felt-tip sketch by Margaret Corbin

and sketching. If you wish to add water-colour to your drawing, be sure that your ink is water-resistant. Draw on cartridge paper, perhaps in a sketch-book.

If you feel unnerved by your clean white sheet of paper you could rough in a few lines of composition with a pencil, but do not overdo this; try to get going with your pens as soon as possible. You may need to draw some of your lines several times before you feel you have got them right and this often results in a feeling of movement and vitality.

When considering how to deal with the different tonal areas you could use the traditional hatching and cross-hatching, ie, a lot of fine parallel lines drawn formally or freely across the particular area. Look back at the various suggestions made about stitching in Chapter 1; exercise 5. Think in terms of stitchery as you draw, so that this time, instead of 'drawing with your needle', you could 'stitch with your pen!' Pen-drawing lends itself very well to the portrayal of textural detail, eg of stone or brick walls, tree bark, wood-grain, leaves, grass, etc. However, do not lose sight of just what depth of tone you are trying to portray.

Another way of dealing with tonal areas is to paint them in over the pen lines using water-colour washes in various tones of grey or in colour.

Alternative pens to those suggested include dip-in pens and felt-tips. An old-fashioned dip-in pen has a pliable nib offering flexibility of line, which is nice to use: the disadvantage is in having to handle a bottle of ink, with the possibility of the odd blot on the paper. If you possess such a pen and some Indian ink, try them out and see if you prefer them.

Felt-tipped pens come in many colours and are very handy, but they can sometimes produce rather crude results and it is difficult to achieve a good range of light to dark tones. It might be interesting, though, to add a grey and one colour when working on a drawing with black pens.

USING CHARCOAL, CONTÉ CRAYON, OR CHALK

These drawing materials all require large-scale working, because they are not suitable for small and refined lines. Do not be discouraged by this; large-scale work often helps people to shed their inhibitions about drawing.

If these materials are new to you, make a start by using chalk and charcoal on a full-sized sheet of grey sugar-paper, or certainly one no smaller than A2. Sooner or later you will also need a drawing-board or large piece of hardboard cut in relation to paper sizes, or big pastry board, etc.

The working set-up needs to be thought out in advance and will make all the difference to your enjoyment and the results you obtain. You should be able to see your subject easily, support the drawing-board comfortably and have your drawing materials ready to hand.

Depending on where the subject is placed, eg on the floor, a stool, a table, etc, you will need to sit so that you can see it easily, with your board propped against a secure support such as the edge of a table, back of a chair, the ironing-board, or an easel. You may prefer to work flat on a table-top, in which case it is better to stand.

Remember to try and draw by moving your arm from the shoulder, encouraging broad flowing movements. You can draw with the point, such as it is, or the side of a smallish piece of chalk or charcoal.

What will you draw? Even a small object like a clothes-peg, an open zip-fastener, or a pair of scissors can look quite exciting when drawn to fill the paper. Take a top-view of the object and make thoughtful use of your black charcoal and white chalk on the grey paper.

Another exercise is to take a close-up view looking down into a smallish bowl or box of pebbles, eggs, cotton reels, etc. Next, draw some fabric draped on the wall, a bowl of fruit or a heap of magazines on the floor, etc. Such drawings may not translate directly into embroidery, but they will extend your confidence and capabilities in drawing, which will also transfer into your handling of other media.

Another interesting way of using charcoal is to work on a slightly smaller piece of cartridge paper, covering all or nearly all the paper with tones of grey or black, then 'draw' with a rubber (an eraser) to create light tones and patterns of white lines, adding lines in black too, as and when it seems appropriate. See *Sea and Sky* on page 165. Work from a simple group of objects which present interesting patterns and variations of light and dark tones.

Conté crayons are more permanent and also more capable of definition than charcoal, and can be used on a slightly smaller scale. They offer rich dark blacks, with the possibility of making all kinds of textural marks, and are thus a very satisfying medium to use on cartridge or sugar-paper.

PASTELS

These can be used for drawing in line, texture or solid colour on cartridge or sugar-paper and can be mixed or overlaid very effectively. The small boxes of colours can be very restricting: they offer no green remotely like the colour of trees or grass and struggling to mix the right colour can be very frustrating. If you enjoy this medium very much it is worth accumulating a good range and variety in every colour.

GOUACHE AND POSTER-COLOUR PAINTS

The dictionary describes gouache as 'a way of painting in opaque colours ground in water and thickened with gum and honey'; poster colour is a humbler and less expensive version of the same thing and likely to be quite adequate for our purposes. As these are water-bound paints, they are easy to use and dry quickly; a slight drawback is that they dry lighter than they look when wet. They are bought either in tubes or pots and should be used thickly, but mixed with a little water if necessary, to produce an opaque layer. When one layer is dry another can be painted on top of it. This medium has its own character, offering plenty of scope, and does not require any great technical proficiency.

Materials required
Basic range of colours
   black, white
   reds – crimson and vermilion
   blues – ultramarine and prussian
   yellows – lemon and chrome
Useful additions
   turquoise
   violet
   cerise
   yellow ochre
   raw and burnt sienna
   Shops also offer a standard red, yellow and blue. These are the colours considered to work most successfully in the

Cyclamen
Chalk and charcoal drawing – a
good technique for confidence
building

colour circle to give good complementary colours and also, when mixed together, to produce a near black. However, the colours listed above can be mixed together, eg crimson and vermilion, to give a good middle red, and this applies to the blues and yellows too. Crimson and ultramarine will give a better purple than vermilion and prussian, but the way to check this is to spend a little time trying out different mixtures of paint.

Brushes   Sable brushes are very nice to use as they are

Paris Cafe and *Sea Creatures,*
poster paint drawings

springy and come to a fine point when wet. They are quite expensive but there are cheaper alternatives available. Try to collect brushes in several sizes, including a fine one. Large hog-hair brushes are useful for working freely and on a large scale. A stencil brush is very good for producing graded colour and textures; they come in several sizes too.

Paper   Cartridge paper or sugar-paper.

Other requirements

    A water jar

    A large plate or piece of hardboard painted white for a palette

    Rags or kitchen paper for wiping brushes and making sure they are quite clean before dipping them into another colour.

Experiment by mixing colours and by adding white or black or both (see the colour exercise on page 26.) Try painting in flat areas and also by dabbing colours freely.

A stencil brush offers interesting possibilities. It should not be dipped in water before use, but touched into fairly thick paint and worked on some scrap paper until it is producing fine powdery marks when you hold it upright and bang it down quite hard on the paper. Try making a stencil by cutting a hole in a piece of paper and laying this over your work. Using your brush, try to grade the tone, making it strong and dark by tapping the brush hard over the edges of the stencil, then fading it gradually; lift a corner of the stencil to see the effect. This method will also work on smooth fabrics, using fabric paints.

WATER-COLOUR by Margaret Corbin

Water-colour gives a full range of colour but with very gentle, subtle changes. It has a transparency not seen in other media.

Materials required

Colours   These come in pans or tubes. Most beginners feel happier with pans – but they will dry out in time. Most professional artists use tubes. There are usually two qualities of paint – 'students' and 'artists'. The artists' colours are the best but they are dearer. Do not buy cheap boxes of paints aimed at the children's market.

Basic starter colours

    one cold yellow (lemon or similar)

    one middle red – scarlet

    one middle blue – ultramarine

These will give a limited range of greens, oranges, purples, browns and greys.

Useful additions

    a warmer yellow – chrome (medium)

    a darker red – crimson

    an orange/red – vermilion, cadmium

    a cold blue – prussian, cerulean

These colours will provide better mixing possibilities and give a fuller range of greens, purples, etc. If you feel the need for green, add veridian or emerald.

Yellow ochre is a useful colour, though somewhat opaque. If you need browns look at the full range of siennas and umbers (burnt and raw).

Black is not really necessary and is disliked by many artists.

White should not be needed either. But it does exist. Use it only as white. Do not mix with other colours or you will lose the transparency that is the special quality of water-colour.

If you are very interested in flowers you will probably need to buy magenta and purple. But beware – many of the sharp pink colours are 'fugitive', ie, they will fade in bright light.

Brushes Start with one small, one medium and one large brush. (Small sizes 1-4, medium 5-8, large 9 onwards.) The best are sable hair and very expensive. Quite adequate are modern synthetic brushes, which are much cheaper. Add other sizes and different shapes later if you become 'hooked'.

Paper The thicker (heavier) the better. Thin papers cost less but buckle when wetted and should be taped to a board so that they dry flat. Thick papers do not need stretching unless used in very large sizes. Surfaces vary and only experience will tell you which you prefer.

Palettes Paint-box lids, white plastic palettes, china palettes (for studio use, they are too heavy for taking on sketching expeditions) and ordinary household plates and saucers. Whatever you use, keep it very clean.

Other requirements Plenty of clean water in clean containers. Do not be lazy in this respect.

Method

There is no definite method. You must experiment and find out what works best for you.

You can wet the paper, either all of it or a certain area of it before applying colour. If you use wet paper, colours will mingle and run and often give pleasant accidental effects. If you paint on the dry paper be sure the paint you mix is wet enough. You can achieve sharp, neat edges in this way. Use a brush soaked in clean water to soften edges you wish to be soft. Do this before the paint dries. Most artists work on a slightly sloping board. You will soon find out at which angle you like to work. To achieve rich, dark colours you need to be generous in the amount of paint you use, but it must still be wet enough to run a little. If you work on a sloping board the surplus paint will collect at the bottom of the painted area. This can be soaked up on to a half-dry brush gently held at the lowest point of the 'blob'.

Water-colour is not suitable for large areas of flat colour. These are more easily obtained with gouache or designers' colours. Allow your water-colour to do as it wishes and make use of the subtleties gained in this way.

It is possible to paint one layer of paint over another. Allow the first wash to dry before adding the second. If, however, you overpaint too many times you will lose the initial 'freshness'. It is sensible to apply the dark colours last – unless you are very certain of where you want the dark bits to be. But you cannot paint over the dark bits. Alterations are possible. Using a slightly stiffer bristled brush you can remove some colours. After thorough drying you can overpaint although if the paper has been damaged the colour may 'run' at the edges. White accents can be put in by 'scratching out' with a knife or point, but only if the paper is thick enough.

When painting do not think too much of the eventual

Rocks by the Sea, a watercolour by Margaret Corbin

design you wish to make, do the painting for its own sake. Afterwards, look at all your paintings and select those, or parts of them, that offer ideas for design. Whatever you paint you can always find a small area that will lend itself to a possible enlargement and a future development as a design.

COLLAGE – with cut or torn paper

We have already considered the use of fabric collage in Chapter 1, and also in the designing of blackwork, using different densities of tone cut from newspapers. Here is another way of building a design in colour by assembling pieces of paper cut or torn from old magazines, colour supplements, tissue-paper, etc. The advantage is the directness of the method, with plenty of colours, textures and perhaps unusual colour relationships to hand which may send you off in new directions. Stick the pieces down on a paper background using wallpaper paste; if you have second thoughts about the design, it is very easy to build it up further by sticking more papers on top. You can also work into it by drawing with a pen, or adding paint, spatter, bits of grass, twigs, etc.

Collage of found materials (assemblage)

A collage can also be built up in a three-dimensional way, using cardboard boxes, cotton reels, card cylinders, polystyrene, string, etc. If this fires your imagination it can be translated into an embroidery by reconstructing your design, this time covering all the units with fabrics and appropriate stitchery, wrapping, needleweaving, etc (see the section on manipulation etc, in Chapter 2).

Jugs and Teapots, a collage of rubbings in Conté crayon

Three pen drawings of a house
by Barbara Siedlecka

USING A SKETCH-BOOK

Keeping a sketch-book is a helpful way of recording your observations. If it contains cartridge paper it can be used for any of the media discussed in this section.

A sketch-book can be very versatile(it can be used for rapid water-colour sketches (to capture a cloudscape), for detailed studies (of roof-tiling, market stalls, waterfalls, a plant), for a piece of work already under way, or for making notes on things of interest (when visiting an exhibition, with written comments about the colours, etc, to jog your memory in the future).

You may feel happier using odd sheets of paper of various sizes and colours, clipped to a board or stiff card. This is a less tidy way of working perhaps, but the really important aspect is that of looking and recording, so do not despise the scribbled note on the back of an envelope.

Ask yourself what seems most important about the scene before you; is it the colour, the effect of light and shade, the shapes, sense of movement, the texture or the general feeling and atmosphere? Try to record this special quality in your sketch.

PHOTOGRAPHY

A photographer once described his work as 'a celebration of noticing'. He recorded all sorts of odd things we often look at without seeing and his searching eye selected some extra-ordinary images.

When we take a photograph we look, select and record, so the picture is a memento of an occasion as well as a useful piece of information – it is our own picture. Some people fear that working from photographs is 'cheating', but creating a design from any mode of recording demands considerable selection and simplification, and translating this into the medium of embroidery takes the whole operation yet a step further away from copying. (See the section on working from a photograph of a landscape in Chapter 1.)

CHAPTER 7

PRESENTATION

The way in which a piece of work is presented will make all the difference to its effectiveness. Whichever mode you choose should be carried out in a professional way and with permanence in mind. In years to come cleaning may be necessary, so it should be possible to remove the work from its mount and to replace it successfully. Adhesives and adhesive tape deteriorate and can damage the fabric, so should be avoided whenever possible.

PREPARATION

Firstly, the work must be stretched on a board as described in Chapter 1. If the result is less than perfect repeat the process until you are satisfied.

Next, cut four long strips of paper and lay one on each side of the work to frame it while it is still on the board. Move them until you have determined exactly the right size and shape of your image, then pin them in place. Stand the work upright and check the placing from a distance, then mark the area with pins, measure it and make a note of the dimensions. When the work is removed from the board, tack out the shape.

SOME MODES OF PRESENTATION

Unless you have already done so, a decision must now be made as to the best form of presentation; five different ways are detailed below.

1 Mounting on firm card or hardboard, for framing
The choice of card or hardboard for the mount would relate to scale, ie, card (preferably acid-free) for a small picture and the extra strength of hardboard for a larger one. Check that the corners are true right-angles and smooth down the hardboard edges with sandpaper. Remember that the frame will need to be slightly larger than the mount, to allow for the thickness of the fabric.

You may already have used a cotton backing to your work but, if not, it is a good idea to put a layer of white cotton sheeting, calico, etc, between the embroidery and the hardboard, both to protect the work from the edges of the hardboard and to diminish its dark colour. Leave a margin of at least 1in (2.5cm) for a small panel, and about 2in (5cm) for a large one, all round the outside of your tacked shape, then cut away the surplus fabric. Cut the backing cotton to the same size, press it, then tack the two fabrics together.

Lay your embroidery face-downwards on a clean table and place the hardboard in position on top of it. Fold over the longer edges on the tacked lines and, using a large needle, thread it with some strong but fine string from a ball, letting the ball roll freely at your feet. Starting above one edge of the hardboard, stitch to and fro from one side to the other, leaving a gap between the stitches of 2-3in (5-7.5cm) according to the size of the panel, until you reach the other end. Keep drawing more thread from the ball as you work. Fasten off at one end, then gradually pull the string tight until the work is

very smooth but not too tight, checking that your tacked lines are straight along the edges of the board, then fasten off. Now fold over the shorter ends, trimming away unnecessary fabric at the corners, and work across in the same way. You may prefer to mitre the corners, depending on the type of fabric used. Now remove the tacking threads and the work is ready for its frame.

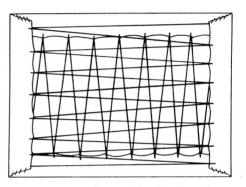

Mounting work on card or hardboard

2 As above, but adding a card window-mount
The tacked line round your design will give you the dimensions for the 'window' within your card mount, so you will need to decide how wide the mount should be, remembering to allow a deeper margin at the bottom. Now cut your card window-mount – the hardboard should be fractionally smaller to allow for the thickness of fabric. It will be necessary to add the dimensions of the window-mount round the edges of your embroidery and to mark them with a tacked line, plus the extra fabric for pulling over the edges of the hardboard. Follow the same procedures as given for 1) above.

Using glass
Glass may be used in either of the above ways of mounting. The advantage is the protection of the work, the disadvantage the reflections in the glass. Non-reflective glass is available, but it produces a blurred effect. Glass also makes a panel heavy and difficult to transport for exhibition purposes. Clear acetate or perspex are possible alternatives.

If the work is padded, or beads, thick texture, etc, used, it may be necessary to insert narrow strips of wood or thick card round the edges and joined at the corners to lift the glass above the surface of the work, and the frame made in relation to this.

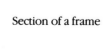 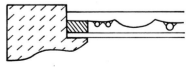

Section of a frame

3 Mounting on a wooden stretcher
To make the wooden stretcher, four strips of wood will be required, approximately 1in (2.5cm) in section, for a panel of about 39in (1m) square, but depending on the required size

and on the weight of the fabric. It must be strongly constructed and reinforced with extra struts if necessary.

Stretch and measure the embroidery as usual and allow 2in (5cm) extra on each edge for wood of 1in (2.5cm) in section, to stretch over the edge and the under-side of the wood.

Fasten the fabric in position with drawing-pins, then fix it to the back of the stretcher using a staple gun, working to about 2in (5cm) from each corner. Now continue tacking each side, keeping the fabric taut, and finally fold the side edge flat across the top and tack it in place. Fold and crease the top edge exactly on the top corner and, after cutting away unnecessary thickness of fabric, tack it in place on the back. Using a tiny slip-stitch work along the corner join as invisibly as possible.

Some people like to mount their work on a permanent frame as soon as any machine stitching has been completed. As previously stated, this is certainly advisable for heavily padded trapunto quilting. It also helps if you are working with very long stitches, but remember you must be able to reach to the middle quite comfortably!

4 Mounting on hardboard raised on a wooden edging
A piece of hardboard will warp unless it is very small. Reinforcing the edges with wooden strips on the back will both prevent warping and provide a neat edge of chosen depth over which the background fabric can be stretched. This gives a feeling of unity and solidity as the work stands out from the wall surface. It is also a simple method which does away with the difficulties of actual framing; very useful if you are a prolific worker.

If the depth is quite shallow, strips of carefully chosen fabric, velvet ribbon, etc, of like depth can be stitched round the edge. If appropriate this panel can be superimposed on a similar but larger one, covered with a suitable material, and the same fabrics, ribbons, etc, repeated round this edge too.

Screw eyes or other fixings can be fastened into the wood at either side within this mount, so the work will lie flat against the wall.

5 Superimposing a window-mount of card covered with fabric
This method offers possibilities for extending the design on to the mount.

The window-mount may, of course, just be covered with a piece of carefully selected fabric, eg some velvet surrounding a canvaswork panel. Alternatively an aspect of the design could be echoed in stitchery, or a border pattern created; it could be padded or quilted, wrapping used, etc.

If you plan to embroider the mount it will need to be designed to enhance the work, not to dominate or compete with it. The size must be carefully planned as must the method by which you intend to cover the window-mount.

Covering card with fabric is not easy. If you cut away the window opening from the fabric, leaving edges to turn under, you are faced with the problem of weak corners, though this can sometimes be overcome with some ingenuity, depending on the type of fabric used. Mitred corners may give better results (see overleaf).

When you are ready to cover the card window-mount, you will need to decide how best to attach the fabric to the mount and the mount to the embroidery. The fabric covering the card could either be stitched in position on the back using a fine but strong thread, in the same way as for mounting fabric

on hardboard, or by using an adhesive sparingly on the back. The mount could then be joined to the outer edges of the embroidery by neat stitching, or with the use of Velcro, or the outer edges carried over to the back of the embroidery and stitched into place.

This particular type of presentation lends itself to all types of panel shapes, both formal and free.

MAKING A WALL-HANGING

Sometimes a piece of work will look well if allowed to hang freely from a support across the top; this approach often enhances the soft look of fabric. It is generally used for patchwork and quilts intended for walls, for felt panels and, of course, tapestries, but is not necessarily confined to these areas. It is likely to work well where there is an even distribution of weight, which might not be the case in a richly embroidered panel.

For patchwork wall-hangings the top edge can be supported by a thin strip of wood, 1¼in (3cm) deep and slightly less wide than the hanging. This is contained in a sleeve of fabric stitched on to the lining just below the top. Screw eyes are inserted through the fabric into the batten near each end and hang on picture-hooks attached to the wall. In this way the support does not show. Some people, however, prefer to hang their work from a pole of wood or metal using strips of fabric, or large rings.

Instructions for making a double border are given, as this method is my personal preference. The borders can be equal or unequal in widths and are applied by the log-cabin method.

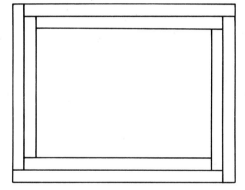

Log cabin borders

1 Adding a cotton backing
Measure the work, then add the full width of the borders (plus turnings) to the length and the same to the width. This will give the size for the cotton backing. Press it, then lay the work on top, right side up, leaving equal margins all round and smoothing it carefully so both fabrics are quite flat. Tack the work in place.

2 Joining the backing to the fabric
Turn the work over so the backing is uppermost. Smooth the fabrics again, then attach them to each other using a few loose oversewing stitches at regular intervals (placed where there are seams in the embroidery so they will not show on the front). The stitches are loose to allow the fabrics to move during variations of temperature or humidity.

3 Tacking out the actual size of the work
Lay the work right side up on a large table or the floor, and

measure the exact position where the borders are to be placed. Mark with pins at frequent intervals and check that the corners are square, then tack out the rectangle.

4 Preparing the borders
a) The inner borders.
Having selected your fabric, and decided on the width of borders you wish to use, add turnings to this measurement and cut four such strips. Two will need to be the length of the tacked rectangle, plus the width of one border, plus a turning allowance at each end. The other two will be as wide as the rectangle, again adding the width of one border and the turnings.

b) The outer borders
Cut or tear four strips of the second fabric. These need to be about twice the chosen width so they can be turned under to neaten the back. This time, two strips need to be the length of the tacked rectangle plus the first border, plus the double width of the second border and one turning allowance. The strips for the width will require a similar addition to those of the length.

Press under one turning allowance down the length of each strip.

5 Adding the inner borders
Place the work right side up on a large table or board that will take drawing-pins. Lay a long strip face-downwards over the design, with the pressed hem touching the tacked line and allowing a turning at the top. Do the same with the other long strip, but this time allow the turning at the bottom.

As the work hangs it will gradually stretch downwards. To prevent this, it needs to be stretched lengthwise, fastened down with drawing-pins, and the borders added a little loosely. This is especially important if you happen to be applying borders of a man-made fabric such as dupion, which will not stretch, to a natural fabric like cotton, which will.

Open out the hem on each border and insert plenty of pins at right-angles to the length, ensuring meanwhile that the pressed line stays exactly on the tacking. Machine stitch along this line, including the turning, and for the precise length of the rectangle. Remove the pins and press the borders into position.

Now add the top and bottom borders, tucking the turning allowance under the long (loose) end of the lengthways strip, and machining right across to the end. Finally, stitch the loose strips in place and press the work.

6 Adding the outer borders
Measure the required width of the inner borders and mark with pins, then add the outer borders following the same procedures as before. Next, measure the correct width of the outer borders, first marking with pins and then tacking through border and backing. Fold the fabric under on this line, pin again and press the edge under.

7 Finishing the corners
Turn the work over and trim together the border and backing fabrics, then mitre the corners. To do this, push a pin through the exact point of the corner, then open it out and mark the pin point with a pencil on the white backing. Draw a diagonal line through this point, tack it through both fabrics, then cut away the fabrics ¼in (0.5cm) below the line. Next, fold the

fabric at the pin-point dot, keeping the two edges together. Pin and machine along the tacked line.

Turn this right side out, pushing scissor points in gently to ensure a neat corner. Press. Repeat for each corner.

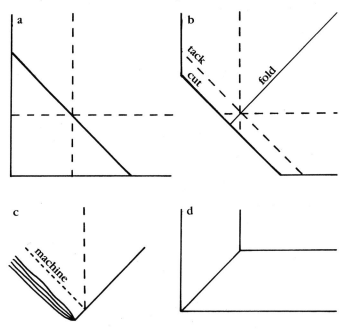

Mitring corners

8 Securing the border on the wrong side
Smooth and flatten the edges into position in relation to the tacked and pressed edge. Pin them in place, then work all the way round securing the edges with a fairly large herringbone stitch, making sure that the edges of the backing fabric are also held quite firmly and that your stitches do not go through to the front of the work.

9 Adding the lining and a sleeve for the batten
The final stage is to neaten the back with curtain lining. On a large hanging take the lining up to ½in (1.5cm) below the top, 1in (2.5cm) in from the sides and about 1½in (4cm) short of the bottom. To prevent pulling it is also advisable to allow extra material across the width, about ⅜in per foot (1 in 30cm), and a little on the length also. When you have worked out the dimensions of the lining, cut it out and press the turnings under.

Cut your strip of wood, or batten, slightly shorter than the width of the hanging and prepare a sleeve for it. To do this, cut another strip of lining material 1in (2.5cm) longer than the batten. The width of the strip is determined by measuring the depth of the wood plus twice its thickness, then adding a turning on either side. Machine a small hem at each end of the strip and press the turnings under.

Pin the strip across near the top of the lining and machine it in position. Lay the wood in place and pin the fabric tightly just below it. Remove the wood and stitch across the lower part of the sleeve; check that the batten will slide in and out.

Pin the lining in place as planned, allowing a fullness at the bottom and slip stitch it all the way round. Now hand stitch the base line of the sleeve through to the cotton backing, taking care to avoid catching the face of the work.

After removing all tacking threads, give the wall-hanging a final press, insert the wooden batten; fix the screws in place and the job is done!

BIBLIOGRAPHY

EMBROIDERY STITCHES

	100 Embroidery Stitches (J & P Coats 1967)
Beaney, Jan	*Stitches, New Approaches* (Batsford, 1987) Shows lively ways of using stitches.
Howard, Constance	*Book of Stitches* (Batsford, 1979)
Snook, Barbara	*Embroidery Stitches* (Dryad, 1985)
Thomas, Mary	*Mary Thomas's Dictionary of Embroidery Stitches* (Dryad, 1985)

DESIGN

Beaney, Jan	*Art of the Needle* (Century, 1989) Design procedures and helpful section on use of silk paints and fabric dyes.
Beck, Thomasina	*Embroiderer's Garden* (David & Charles, 1988)
Campbell-Harding, Valerie	*Faces and Figures in Embroidery* (Batsford, 1985) Offers a variety of ways of looking and working.
Embroiderer's Guild	*Designer Textiles* (David & Charles, 1987)
Howard, Constance	*Inspiration for Embroidery* (Batsford, 1989)
Whyte, Kathleen	*Design in Embroidery* (Batsford, 1983) The above two seminal books were written in the 1960s and still offer a great breadth of ideas.
Itten, Johannes	*Design and Form* (Thames and Hudson, 1987) The basic course at the Bauhaus.
de Sausmarez, Maurice	*Basic Design: The Dynamics of Visual Form* (Studio Visa/Van Nostrand Reinhold, 1964)

COLOUR

Howard, Constance	*Embroidery and Colour* (Batsford, 1986)

ETHNIC WORK

Broadbent, Moira	*Animal Regalia* (Portia Press, Whitchurch, 1985) Available from the author at Holly Lodge, How Green, Chipstead, Surrey.
Singer, Margo and Spyrou, Mary	*Textile Arts – Multicultural Traditions* (A & C Black 1989) Useful, demonstrates a variety of methods and techniques.

METHODS

de Dillmont, Therese	*Encyclopaedia of Needlework* (Bracken Books, 1987)
Thomas, Mary	*Embroidery Book* (Hodder & Stoughton, 1989)

MATERIALS

Evers, Inge	*Felt-making – Techniques and Projects* (A & C Black, 1987)
Freeman, Sue	*Felt Craft* (David & Charles, 1988)
Littlejohn, Jean	*Fabrics for Embroidery* (Batsford, 1986) Imaginative explorations using a wide variety of materials.

COUNTED METHODS

McNeill, Moyra	*Drawn Thread Embroidery* (Batsford, 1989)
—	*Pulled Thread* (Joseph Ward, Dewsbury, 1988)
Pascoe, Margaret	*Blackwork Embroidery* (Batsford, 1989)
Rhodes, Mary	*Dictionary of Canvas Work Stitches* (Batsford, 1980)
—	*Ideas for Canvas Work* (Batsford, 1984)

MACHINE EMBROIDERY

Butler, Anne	*Machine Stitches* (Batsford, 1976)
Clucas, Joy	*The New Machine Embroidery* (David & Charles, 1987)
McNeill, Moyra	*Machine Embroidery – Lace and See-Through Techniques* (Batsford, 1989) Helpful on vanishing and dissolvable materials.
Risley, Christine	*Machine Embroidery* (Studio Vista, 1973)

PATCHWORK AND QUILTING

Chase, Pattie and Dolbier, Mimi	*The Contemporary Quilt – New American Quilts and Fabric Art* (E. P. Dutton, New York, 1978)
Colby, Averil	*Patchwork* (Batsford, 1987)
James, Michael	*The Quiltmaker's Handbook: A Guide to Design and Construction* (Prentice Hall, 1978)
Short, Eirian	*Quilting: technique, design and application* (Batsford, 1985)

LETTERING

Russell, Pat	*Lettering for Embroidery* (Batsford, 1985)

WEAVING

Hecht, Ann	*The Art of the Loom* (British Museum Publication, 1989)

PAINTING ON SILK

Kennedy, Jill and Varrell, Jane	*Painting on Silk* (Dryad, 1988)

DRAWING

Box, Richard	*Drawing and Design for Embroidery* (Batsford, 1989)
Chaet, Bernard	*The Art of Drawing* (Holt, Rinehart and Winston, 1970)

CREATIVITY

P. E. Vernon (Ed)	*Creativity* (Penguin, 1970) Includes article by G. Wallas on creativity.

INDEX

ACKNOWLEDGEMENTS

Many thanks to Joan Edwards for suggesting that I write this book, and to those who contributed embroideries, drawings, prints or other work.

To the group of Surrey teachers who worked on some of my projects, and to Andrew Leah and his staff at the NE Surrey Staff Development Centre.

To Margaret Corbin for her piece on water-colour painting.

To Dudley Moss for photographing the most awkward pieces, to Keith Harding of Goodness Gracious for the majority of the colour photography, and to Jim Pascoe for all the black and white prints.

To Shirley Cave and Word Perfect for their care in putting my text on word processor, often at short notice.

To Anne Joyce and staff at the Embroiderers' Guild for assistance and encouragement at Hampton Court.

Finally, thanks to Peter, my husband, for drawing up all the diagrams, and for his patient help and support at every stage of the book.